THE STRANGE GIFT OF ESTRANGEMENT

The Strange Gift of Estrangement

Hope for Grieving Parents of Estranged Adult Children

SHEILA TEXEIRA

Sheila Texeira

CONTENTS

DEDICATION

Dedicated to Mark, the love of my life, without whose continuous love and support this book could not have been written, and Calvin, my one and only grandchild, a child I may likely never meet but whom I love with all my heart.

INTRODUCTION

I am so tired of all the negativity around me! Are you? This world is toxic, and it is sick. I hate watching the news, reading the newspaper or even interacting with my neighbors. I don't want to appear antisocial. I genuinely love people. But this world has made us cold and cruel, and nowhere is this most evident as with the estrangement of our own adult children.

There is a disturbing trend of young adults abandoning their parents for otherwise innocuous reasons. As of 2023, it is currently estimated that 1 in 8 older parents are estranged from an adult child. This trend is fueled by various websites and mental health practitioners that encourage adult children to go, "no contact", or "NC". They are told they are brave for protecting themselves from the "toxic narcissists", that are their parents. The somehow believe that the people that have devoted their lives to protecting them from harm, are the very ones inflicting this "harm".

The result is a society of unhappy people. Well over 50% of all marriages end in divorce. Well over 50% of all young adults do not even believe in marriage. We need to get back to the days where it was easy to talk to strangers and politeness was as natural as breathing. Back to the days where people believed in love and looked out for their neighbors. We need to start loving ourselves again. We each need to be the change we wish to see in the world. We need to heal ourselves and start loving ourselves, and the people who truly love us, again.

While we have no control over the thoughts and actions of others, we do have control over ourselves, our reactions, our choices, and essentially the person we are meant to evolve into. Like a phoenix rises from the ashes to transform into a new more glorious version of the old self, we too must look past our suffering at the hands of our heavily manipulated adult children and become greater. This is our gift. We have been given a tremendous opportunity to discover ourselves and once again chase the dreams that we left behind in our childhood minds and exchanged for the parent persona that society demanded of us. That persona which left much of our life void of dreams, aspirations, and even self-expression. We wore mom jeans and developed dad bods. We coached sports we deplored and volunteered for excruciating assignments in our children's school and extra-curricular activities.

Happy people are successful people. This is simply because being happy makes it easy to stay motivated to reaching your goals. Your thoughts have a very significant impact on the life you lead and the quality of the relationships you will have with family members, friends, and significant others. Some even reason that our thoughts and beliefs can have an even stronger effect on our health than modern medicine. Consider these examples:

• A middle-aged man dies a day after his doctor diagnosed him with Cancer, even though his autopsy revealed he was misdiagnosed.

• Many women who are desperate to have a child will begin to have real symptoms of a pregnancy such as cravings and an increase in the size of their breasts, even though they are not actually pregnant.

• People who suffer from Depression and participate in clinical trials for new antidepressants start experiencing an improvement in their moods although they were given the placebo and not the actual drug.

It has been scientifically proven that you can improve your health, career and relationships simply by improving the way you think about yourself and the world around you. This is a lot cheaper than paying for sessions with a therapist or paying a Divorce Lawyer. This book is intended to help you heal yourself of all the scars and the influence of all the negativity around. I guarantee that learning to rid yourself of the pain of this estrangement, will drastically improve the quality of your life from this point forward. Please note that from this point forward, I will only rarely mention "they who shall not be named". The purpose is that this book is not about them. It's about you.

~ 1 ~

WHAT'S HAPPENING

What's Happening? First and foremost, the decision of your adult children to go no contact with you, or some form of NC, was not your fault. You likely did everything in your power to be the best mom/dad/grandma/grandpa on the face of the planet. I know you did, because I did too. Heck, even my ex-husband who hates me, admits I was a great mother.

I know this because in my experience, those people who were abused during their childhood, continue seeking their parent's love and attention for the remainder of their lives.

A friend of mine told me the story of her childhood which started out with her mother abandoning her as a 2-week-old infant. Her mother simply walked away, leaving her crying in her crib without any other caregiver or anyone even knowing the child was unsupervised. The neighbors heard her cries and knew her mother was not home. As time went on, they realized that her mother was not returning anytime soon and called police. Her mother had no intention of ever returning. My friend's biological father was found, and custody was given to him, but he had a life of his own and a newborn didn't really fit his style. She was neglected and abused. I'll spare the graphic details, but her life was pure HELL from day one.

My friend has found her mother many times over the years. Her mother has severe mental health issues, if that isn't already

6

apparent, so when life gets to be too much for her, she simply walks away, finds a new town and starts over. Each time I talk to my friend, one of the first things she mentions is her mom, "I found her again', or "I haven't seen her for X number of months". "Girl, she left you for dead, she doesn't care about you, move on", I scream quietly to myself, while verbally feigning interest in the life of a woman that I detest.

But so goes the paradox, of adult children who experienced horrific childhood trauma, continually seeking parental love, and over-indulged princes and princesses tossing away good and loving parents because it's the "in' thing to do, or because one time their parent said something that hurt their feelings.

Please keep in mind there are adults who have gone NC for valid reasons. I, myself have a strained relationship with my parents. I grew up in a home with severe domestic violence, and emotional abuse. I knew from an early age, I was, in my father's own words, "different', "she's not like us", he once told my ex-husband. Truer words have never been spoken. Was I perfect? HELL NO!!! Did I try to be the best I could be? Yes, I did.

~ 2 ~

KNOW THY SELF

Know Thy Self. "The more you know yourself, the more patience you have for what you see in others." - Erik Erikson. Knowing who you are is a very crucial aspect of healing yourself. How can you avoid a disaster if you are simply floating through life with no clear sense of what you stand for, and what you refuse to tolerate? There is a reason why the small-town girl with big dreams, who gets to the big city, often ends up in some miserable and dare I say, compromising, situation.

Think too of the unhappy Doctor who is only a doctor because his parents decided that he needed to become the first Doctor in their family. What about the hen picked mama's boy who dates a girl he cannot stand because it makes his mother happy? These three have a lot in common. Their problem can be explained in the old saying that points out that if we do not know where we are going, any road will be the right one. And better yet, 'if we do not stand for something, we will fall for anything.' In other words, if we do not understand ourselves, this includes our hopes, dreams, and aspirations, it will be easy for just about anyone to push us into a decision we will regret for the rest of our lives. Living down a choice you regret, especially if you must face its consequences daily, is going to be one of the hardest things you have ever had to do.

Living with the burden of these choices is part of the reason many people are so bitter and unkind. This is not the way I want you to navigate through your life.

Therefore, I choose to view estrangement as a gift that our estranged adult children have given us. They've given us a chance to return to a happier, healthier mental state. A reset.

When we take the time to understand who we truly are, the intricacies of our own personalities, we will have the keys to unlock our true potential. You cannot become your best self if you do not know what this entails. When you understand yourself, you are more likely to end up choosing a career that you love, or second or even third career that you love. And it is quite easy to be passionately driven to achieve great things when you are pursuing a career that you love. Additionally, when you are at the top of your game, you will seek out the kind of partners and friends that will make you happy and thus bring out the best in you. They will understand the way you think and may very well think the same way you do too. These are the kind of people who will not laugh at your dreams or be jealous of your success. Being surrounded by loving, supportive people, will make you a kinder, happier and dare I say, more successful person.

Individuals who have a deep understanding of themselves, are often more decisive and optimistic. That is because these individuals are in full control of their life choices, and they chose well. They are more likely to see opportunities where others see setbacks. It also takes far less effort to be productive when you enjoy what you do. Additionally, the fact that you enjoy your career will give you a competitive edge and you will not depend on the praise of others for motivation. The satisfaction of a job well done will keep you pushing forward.

I know that these may seem like ideal circumstances, where our choices are not dependent on the desires of our family and where we are all strong enough not to succumb to the pressure, they will put on us to make a certain decision. But believe me, knowing and truly understanding yourself will open doors to opportunities you would have never seen coming otherwise. It will be easier for you to stand up to the pressures around you when you know without a doubt what the right decision for you will be. I am not encouraging you to shrug your responsibilities of providing for your family, I am encouraging you to understand who you are and be true to who you are always. You will be much happier as a result, and far easier to love, when you are not carrying the heavy weight of a bad decision around for the rest of your life.

How to Get to Know Yourself

This is easier said than done, but it is not impossible. You can start with some objective assessment. This does not mean simply asking the people around what they think of you. Your interactions with them, whether negative or positive, will prevent them from being as objective as you need them to be. A better option would be making use of a reputable personality test.

One of the popular options is the Myers-Briggs Personality type test. This test will determine which of the 16 personality types of this theory best describes who you are. It has gained popularity in recent times because its results can be used to determine the environment you work best in and even how you interact with the people around you. Plus, whether you like the results or not they tend to be surprisingly accurate.

Career aptitude tests are another great option. These are designed to help you understand your skill set better and how you can use these skills to select the right career. It is never too late to start a career that you can love.

Once you have a carefully thought out your plan that will allow you to care for your responsibilities and still venture into a field that you love, go for it. It might be a case that money is tight, and you are already strapped for time and may not be able to make a move right now. But I would encourage you to continue preparing yourself. Keep learning all that you can about that career online or from the people around you. That way, if the opportunity should arise, you will be able to take it.

Once you have taken the time to learn about yourself, you may find some dirty laundry and hidden scars that you probably would have rather kept hidden. Unfortunately, you have been wearing these scars every day in the way you interact with those around you. These scars could have made you too soft to express how you feel or too cold to care about the feelings of others. Now that you can see yourself clearly, become the best version of yourself. Love yourself. And above all else, be true to yourself. Knowing your limits is another important skill to master in order to navigate through this crazy world successfully. One of those limits must be refusal to tolerate abuse from others, including your children and going "no contact", without valid reasons, is abuse.

~ 3 ~

KNOW THY LIMITS

"A great man is always willing to be little." — Ralph Waldo Emerson

Know your limits. A key aspect of the results of a Myers-Briggs Personality type test is the section which outlines your strengths and weakness. A lot of the mistakes we make and problems we encounter could have been avoided altogether if we were a little more knowledgeable about our limitations. Just think about an eager weightlifter who tries to lift too much, too soon. What do you think will happen? Any rational individual will realize that the weightlifter is going to hurt themselves. Some will argue that this illustration is encouraging us to limit ourselves, and if we do, and stop pushing ourselves, we will never know our true potential.

There is no limit to what you can achieve if you set your mind to it, and sometimes you will never know how strong you are until you try. You need to, however, ensure that reason and logic prevail when reaching out to achieve your goals. If you have never lifted 100 pounds, maybe starting with 20 pounds today would be a better idea. There is nothing wrong with thinking big, but I would encourage you to start small and work your way up. In essence, I am encouraging you to be modest in your expectations.

Modesty will not only help you to avoid setting unrealistic expectations, but it will also help you to set realistic time frames to achieve your goals. Many people become frustrated when they reach a certain age and have not achieved a certain goal. But just consider the contrast between Mark Zuckerberg and Colonel Sanders. Mark Zuckerberg founded his Facebook empire in his early twenties, but Colonel Sanders did not become the founder of Kentucky Fried Chicken (KFC) until he was in his eighty's. Both men are considered highly successful, but each achieved success at different times.

Maybe it's just not your time or maybe you are just not in the right industry. As highlighted previously, choosing a career in a field you love, will help you to stay motivated and become successful. This theory is demonstrated in the lives of both men. Their success was as a result of a passion for something they loved. A modest approach to life will also help you to avoid comparing your achievements to those of other people. Some people hit the ball out of the park on the first try, and there are others who must work their way up the ladder. Some will get married right out of college, others will have to wait a few years and kiss a few, or a few hundred, frogs before they find the right person. In fact, both Mark Zuckerberg and Colonel Sanders experienced many setbacks on the way to success. You will too. Do not expect that your life will be different. No matter what you hope to achieve, you are going to have to work harder than you have ever worked before, and you may have to wait longer than you expected too.

The beautiful quality of modesty extends far beyond becoming successful. This is a quality that will help you to stop biting off more than you can chew. You do not need to say yes to everyone. This applies both to your personal life, and at work. Don't agree to unreasonable deadlines because you want to impress your boss, unless you are 100% sure you will be able to complete the task. If you have been given an assignment, and you are unsure about how to get it done, do not be afraid to ask for help. If you work a full-time job and have a spouse to take care of, don't commit to too much else, including energy spent on estranged adult children, which is truly a waste of precious energy.

Know thy limits! This applies to your time, energy, emotions, and skills. Modesty works hand in hand with honesty, later in this book I will explain you can heal yourself and improve your life by means of this quality as well.

~ 4 ~

BE HONEST

"Honesty is the fastest way to prevent a mistake from turning into a failure." - James Altucher

Be Honest. The only thing worse than a liar is a thief. Liars make life difficult and often do not realize the far-reaching effects of their actions. Lying makes us unhappy people, who constantly must be covering our tracks and watching our backs. In fact, there are few things as toxic as a liar. We should never allow the negativity in this world to force us to become dishonest people. Lying will only put you closer to the door that leads to cheating and stealing. Quit while you are ahead. Just think about the possible outcomes of a single act of dishonesty:
- Permanent damage to your reputation
- Permanent damage to your relationships
- Loss of income
- Loss of self-respect
- Permanently damaging the reputation of another individual
- Feelings of guilt
- Loss of sleep
- Loss of trust

If you know a dishonest person, perhaps it's your own estranged adult child, you should feel pity for them. They are causing themselves a tremendous amount of suffering by choosing dishonesty.

If you research the word honesty, you find synonyms such as honor, sincerity, fairness, integrity, uprightness, virtue and truthfulness. Being honest requires more than not lying when in a difficult situation. Being honest requires being morally upright in all things. In other words, we will try to be truthful in all things and gain the trust of those around us, by means of our actions.

But honesty is a very tricky thing. It is hard to list all the areas in which we need to be honest. A good rule of thumb if you are unsure if an act is honest or not, is whether you must hide it or deceive someone into believing you did otherwise. If you will need to hide or cover your tracks after doing or saying something, you are probably not being honest.

That's not to say that the initial feelings of shame and seeking to hide, that occur in the beginning of estrangement, are due to dishonesty. Those are most often due to gaslighting from dishonest people. If you have been the victim of effective gaslighting, you will feel these same feelings. You may even question reality. These are normal reactions to abuse of this nature.

The benefits of being honest far outweigh any challenges you may perceive as a result of this course of action. Think of the peace of mind of not having to rethink your every move or watching over your shoulder because you are constantly in fear of being found out. Imagine waking up and not being burdened by the heavy guilt as a result of your actions.

And don't be fooled into thinking that no one benefits from your honesty. It is very easy to become attracted to and to respect someone who is honest. Most employers include that quality as being of the utmost importance when seeking new recruits or considering a possible promotion of someone within their organization.

Being honest does not mean that we should volunteer all our confidential affairs to everyone who is trying to pry into our business. Instead, we should not withhold relevant information from individuals who deserve a truthful answer.

Being honest also means avoiding the various means that will pop up to get more than we deserve or leading someone to believe something about ourselves that is not true. There are, however, times when some of us might find ourselves in very catastrophic situations because we are thought of as being too honest. This is often the case when our words are not tempered with kindness.

Later we will explore how that attribute can help us avoid a lot of the problems that can result from that sort of speech.

~ 5 ~

BE KIND

"Kindness is the language which the deaf can hear and the blind can see." - Mark Twain

Being kind means being warm, considerate, gentle and friendly. To get a friend, you must be a friend. Even more cliché is the saying, 'birds of a feather, flock together.' If you want to attract happy, supportive people into your life, you need to be that kind of person. Why would anyone want to be around you otherwise?

As the wise Maya Angelou highlighted, long after the memory of the interaction has faded, people will remember how that interaction made them feel. When we are unkind, we make the lives of those around us much harder than it must be. We make them feel unloved, underappreciated, and isolated when we are mean or unpleasant. Would you want anyone to treat you that way? Would you enjoy such harsh treatment? Don't you think treating people that way at work, at school or in your own home, makes your life a lot harder than it must be as well?

Kindness fosters a spirit of cooperation, even among people who do not really know each other. Surrounding yourself with people who are willing to work alongside you is far easier than trying to conquer this world alone.

Being unkind envelopes a wide variety of actions. Our words are the most common form of unkindness. Being harsh, condescending or even abrupt, can be interpreted as unkind. Using your words to put others down and elevate yourself is not only unkind, but also a very selfish act, that often causes more harm than good. A key aspect of kindness is being polite. Let us take some time to learn more about this beautiful quality.

Why Be Polite? Being polite is not as hard as some people make it seem. While it is true that being polite is becoming increasingly difficult as a result of the negative attitudes of the people around us, it is not impossible. Being polite might inflate the ego of these individuals, but our being polite in not a reflection on them. Our being polite reflects positively on our character, come what may.

Individuals who are polite are often thought of as kind, principled, professional and pleasant. And with this very interconnected world that we live in, you just never know who you might have insulted. Just imagine how embarrassed you will be if you show up for a job interview, only to realize that the man you just cursed in the parking lot because you think they parked in 'your' spot, is the interviewer. Trust me, it has happened many times before and could happen to you.

Being polite involves being respectful and considerate of the needs, feelings, time, resources, values and cultural norms, of others. Being polite and kind will make you very likable and will encourage others to reciprocate your consideration.

Another benefit of being polite is that it will make it very easy for you to gain the respect of those around you. Even if they do not instantly change their behavior, they will be forced to respect you and your standards. Eventually, they may change for the better as a result of your efforts.

Wouldn't life be much easier if we all had jobs in which our employees, subordinates, colleagues, and family all treated us with respect? Respect must be earned and being polite is one of the easiest ways to earn it.

How to be Polite and Kind

1. If you have nothing kind to say, don't say it, post it on social media or even think it. Even words that are whispered to a friend have been known to turn around and bite you.
2. Don't be stingy with greetings and salutations. If you enter a room, pleasantly greet all present. When you are leavings, kindly excuse yourself. And if you are greeted, respond warmly and with a smile.
3. Do not criticize the efforts of others, especially when it is obvious that they tried very hard to accomplish a particular task. If you must offer some constructive criticism, sandwich it with some genuine commendation.
4. Be appreciative of the efforts of others. Even if what is presented is not to your liking, there is no need to make it known.
5. Try to learn a little about the cultural norms and beliefs of those around you. You do not have to share their views; you simply need to know enough not to unintentionally offend them. It is also most polite to allow them to freely express these views, without fear of being disrespected. You can always agree to disagree.
6. You do not always have to insist on things being done your way. Give someone else a chance to shine every now and then.
7. Don't monopolize conversations by speaking only about yourself and your accomplishments. Show personal interest in others by asking them about themselves and listening to what they have to say.
8. When someone is speaking to you, give them your full attention. Stop walking, typing or whatever else you are doing, and make eye contact. If you are busy, politely pause, evaluate how lengthy the conversations need to be, assure them that you value what they have to say, and then arrange a more suitable time to continue.

~ 6 ~

BE FORGIVING

"The weak can never forgive. Forgiveness is the attribute of the strong."- Gandhi

Sound like someone you know? It is not easy to forgive. The very existence of the need to use the word implies that we have been hurt in some way. Forgiving a grievance, whether real or imagined, will be one of the best gifts you can give yourself. This is so whether you believe the individual deserves such kindness or not.

When we refuse to forgive, we become resentful. Holding on to resentment is like drinking poison and expecting the individual that wronged us to suffer. It can also be compared to inflicting wounds on our own bodies and expecting someone else to feel the pain. This logic is not only riddled with flaws, but also quite dangerous.

Resentment can easily become hate and hatred is a very ugly thing. But why do we find it so hard to forgive? If forgiving someone who hurt us will be so beneficial, why does the very idea of letting go of the hurt make us feel so uneasy?

The real problem lies in the fact that none of us want to continue reliving the horror of whatever wrong was done to us. But as we continue to think about how badly we were hurt, we unconsciously begin to think about making the individual pay for what they did. Our flawed sense of justice often compels us to believe that if we hold on to all the pain that was caused and refuse to let it go, we will be getting the justice we deserve. This is especially so when the individual does not appear to be sorry for what they have done. Unfortunately, we cannot force the anyone, including our estranged adult children, to become a better person by resentfully withholding our love and kindness from them.

We are only hurting ourselves as we force our minds to relive the pain repeatedly. While we are angrily storming through life with the heaviness of resentment in our hearts, our countenance, our speech, and our mood will be adversely affected. Even though we may have been wronged by one or maybe a few of our children, everyone around us will begin to be affected.

Resentment often causes us to be irritable, depressed, and generally very unpleasant. And to make matters worse, it is often the people we love and not the people that wronged us, who will end up suffering as a result of what took place.

The weight of resentment has also been known to affect our memory, productivity at work, ability to perform routine tasks, ability to focus, and even our sex drive. Being bitter and refusing to forgive has also been linked to weakened immune systems, poor heart health, and even high blood pressure.

As you can see, refusing to forgive will never prove beneficial. But what exactly is forgiveness? Is it simply forgetting what took place? Does forgiveness mean we simply pretend that nothing happened? Nope. It is not that simple.

When we forgive, we must involve more than our words. We must change how we think and feel about the individual. It is as if we are allowing them to start with a clean slate all over again. You refuse to allow the situation to cause you, or the parties involved to hurt you any longer. This requires a high level of emotional intelligence, self-control, and love.

Forgiveness is not just "letting them off the hook" for what they did, it is allowing those involved to stop dwelling in the past and move on to more important things.

"Forgiveness means that you fill yourself with love, and you radiate that love outward. You need to refuse to hang onto the venom or hatred that was engendered by the behaviors that caused the wounds." - Wayne Dyer

Becoming that enraged as a result of someone else's actions and allowing yourself to remain upset over what took place for an extended period, is really giving the individual they key to your happiness. It is as if you are allowing that individual to control you, and they will continue to control you until you muster up the courage needed to forgive them.

Forgiveness is also beneficial because it often results when we become aware of our own faults. It becomes easier for us to forgive when we remember that we too have had to ask for forgiveness many times. Contrary to what we may believe, we are not perfect. We sometimes hurt the people around us, even the ones we love, without even realizing it.

When we refuse to harbor resentment and practice forgiveness, it will be easy for those around us to forgive us when we err. Here are a few reasons why it is beneficial to practice being forgiving:

• You will be a lot happier and in a much better mood
• You will sleep better at night
• You will not jeopardize your job by not being productive
• You will not jeopardize your relationship with your significant other or your family
• You will learn greater self-control and self-awareness
• Your will enjoy greater peace
• You will gain the respect of those around you
• You will no longer feel the pain of the damage that was done
• You will experience less anxiety
• Your self-esteem will increase as you observe your own personal strength

What Forgiveness is Not! Being forgiving does not mean you have to be a push over and allow yourself to be hurt repeatedly. While you will let go of any grudge that you may have against the party or parties that wronged you, you certainly do not have to put yourself in a position for you to be hurt that way again. It is perfectly acceptable to be a little more cautious now that you have seen what these people are capable of. But please be very careful. In the case of minor offenses, which are those that were not purposefully malicious, do not make the mistake of assuming that the act represents who the person is. Please remember that we all make mistakes, and we too have caused someone else pain.

Forgiveness is also not an opportunity for revenge. Declaring that you have forgiven someone is not a proclamation that you now have the "upper hand." The persons involved may have been guilty, but they certainly do not owe you anything. Even if they do not apologize, you have still gained quite a lot by extending this peace offering and letting go of the bitterness that once consumed you.

Remember that by being forgiving, you are doing yourself a favor. While they might benefit as a result of your decision, forgiving them is a gift to yourself.

How to Forgive

Because we are both aware that forgiving someone who hurt you is not easy, I would never demand that you do so instantly or all at once. You have the option of forgiving in stages.

Gradually letting go of your resentment towards the individuals who have wronged you, will ensure that you have enough time to root out any trace of the bitterness you have towards them, out of your mind and heart. If you get the opportunity to see this person often, you can start by simply saying hello. This may come as a surprise to them because they were not expecting such a kind gesture, and that might open the way for the discussion you both need to get some closure.

Sometimes, even though you were wronged, it is best to take the initiative to set matters straight. Always remember how this humble act will benefit you in the long run, whether they appreciate the gesture or not.

Another simple exercise that will help us to forgive is writing down the name of the person or persons that hurt you and listing all that they have ever done to upset you. Once you have completed that list, write a list of all the occasions on which you have hurt someone, and had to ask for forgiveness. This is not something that we are inclined to think about. Seeing in black and white how often we have let our bad habits hurt those around us, especially those we love, may be just the push we need to let go of any grudges we may have. What is even more alarming to some individuals is when they see the names of the person, they resent on the list of persons who they have had to ask for forgiveness.

Another useful exercise would be to make a list of all the good things this person has done for you. This exercise will help you to remember that despite their faults, this individual or these individuals, also have many beautiful qualities as well. In the case of those closest to us, these qualities are the very reason why we loved them and kept them close in the first place. Just think, extending the olive branch of peace may even help this person to see the flaw in their thinking and change for the better. You would have made the world a better place by helping just one individual to become a better person.

Such kindness does not go unnoticed, or without reward. It takes a very strong person to be forgiving. But think of how much better our lives would be if we did not walk around with the bitterness of resentment each day.

Letting go of that heavy burden is one of the best ways to heal ourselves. This world was already a catastrophe, and it certainly does not need any more resentment to make it worse. Later we will explore how being generous can also help us become far happier, and more successful people in this world, simply by being generous.

~ 7 ~

BE GENEROUS

"If you can't feed a hundred people, then just feed one."
—Mother Teresa

A generous person is not required to give all their possessions away. A generous person is also not required to allow others to push them around. Being generous involves firstly, the readiness to give or being willing to give more than is required. Being generous takes kindness to the next level.

You might be kind at heart, and often think about helping others, but unless you take them time to get the ball rolling in offering your time, energy or other resources for the benefit of another individual, you have not truly mastered the art of being generous.

Generosity moves us to give of ourselves willingly and expect nothing in return. I know you should be wondering how giving away your assets can help you live a better life. The truth is that many often regard generosity of one of the keys to being truly happy in this miserable world. In fact, many medical practitioners will attest to the fact that being generous is also very good for your health. In fact, here are some of the proven benefits of giving generously:

- Reduced stress
- Lessening the likelihood of suffering from depression
- Increased sense of purpose

- Greater happiness
- Stronger families and marriages
- Less clutter
- Reduced risk of dementia
- Greater appreciation for all that you have
- More likely to benefit from the generosity of others

A generous person often seeks out opportunities to do good for others. Just think about volunteers who make their way to help at Soup Kitchens every weekend. Those of us brave enough to sign up for the Peace Corps are also considered quite generous. But simply helping an elderly lady with her grocery bags or stopping to allow a child to cross the road, can be considered generous. This kind of concern for others proves beneficial because it forces us to focus on the needs of others instead of on our own problems.

Anything that minimizes the effect of our problems, whether in our family or personal relationships or even financially, will have a direct effect on our health. Being generous protects us from all the cynicism and narcissism that makes it so hard to navigate our way through this world.

I would, however, encourage you to be cautious as you endeavor to be more generous. Be very careful of the way in which you demonstrate your generosity. Please be especially careful when being generous to members of the opposite sex. If you are already taken, and you don't want to send the wrong impression, avoid gifts or favors that are personal in nature. A personal gift is anything related to one's body. Perfume, for example, would be considered a personal gift.

Please also bear in mind that your own safety may come into play when being generous. Many people have gotten robbed when asked by a seemingly homeless person to give some money. Reaching into your wallet or bag, and revealing where your cash is kept, and how much cash you have, is a bad idea, no matter how needy the person may appear to be. A safer option would be to let the person know that you will return with a gift. I would strongly suggest that you go to a secure location, one that is away from prying eyes, and package everything that you would like to donate to this individual in advance.

My final word of caution is that you need to feel out the person before being too generous. Some people like spontaneity and others prefer if you first ask them if they need your help. Even the best of intentions can put you in awkward situations if they are not executed correctly.

We have discussed at length, how improving various aspects of your own personality can help you to heal yourself and avoid a lot of the emotional baggage that comes along with the negativity in this world.

~ 8 ~

BE YOURSELF

"Be yourself; everyone else is already taken." — Oscar Wilde

Being yourself. "The greatest gift you ever give is your honest self." — Fred Rogers. We all need to learn to be ourselves again. This is one of the most crucial aspects of successfully navigating through this catastrophe we call life. This encouragement is in no way giving you the right to be a jerk. We have already discussed that healing ourselves from the pain caused by this world requires that we work hard to get rid of our negative traits.

Traits such as being arrogant, rude, dishonest and stingy have no place in your life. When we proudly walk around with these ugly habits, we are inviting all sorts of negativity into our lives. The result of that is only more pain and disappointment. That is why I encouraged you to get to know yourself. This will better equip you to heal yourself, by learning more about your faults.

So, what exactly does it mean to be yourself? It requires that you distance yourself from all the labels the world around us has imposed on us, such as "toxic", "narcissistic" and "abusive". These ugly labels come about because of the way we look, the way we dress or even the community we grew up in. At times, these labels are completely unjustifiable. Historically, nations have used labels to dehumanize specific groups of people, to further a political cause or even to justify genocide. Labels are dangerous.

There is no reason for us to allow the world around us to squeeze us into a mold that doesn't really represent who we are. Just think about how liberating it would be to not have to pretend to be something you are not.

This is all within reason of course. We would never want to take certain liberties that may have far reaching effects on our personal life and may even jeopardize our jobs. That means that you might want to hold off on anything drastic, like dying your hair purple and green, until you find an employer that is willing to accommodate such a choice.

Here are 5 important reasons why you need to start being true to yourself:

1. You will never be able to please everyone. If you constantly allow the people around you to determine who you are, you will constantly have to change what you stand for in order to try and make everyone happy. The only problem with this is that you will be dealing with so many conflicting demands that you will eventually end up disappointing someone. Additionally, putting yourself under this kind of pressure will leave you feeling dissatisfied in the end.

2. The society around us really doesn't know what it wants. The media portrays both the meek homemaker and the fierce go getter, as the ideal woman. Society also demands that men be sensitive to the needs of the opposite sex and the dangerous bad boy as well. Which will you be if you are simply allowing those around you to determine who you are? Whatever you decide to be, just remember that it is quite exhausting to be putting on this kind of show every day.

3. You will end up making life-changing decisions based on the whims of the people around you, who will not suffer the consequences of these choices. If you decide to have a child, simply because your family thinks it's time, you will be the one to have to take care of that child! If you decide to pursue

a career because your peers think you would do well in it, you will have to live with the burden of a career that you hate, forever.

4. The truth always comes out. Sooner or later, people will begin to realize that you are faking. Unfortunately, as we see in the case of many celebrities, the truth often comes out in a big scandal or breakdown.

5. When you are content with who you are, you will be truly happy. How can you love yourself, when you are constantly pretending to be something that you are not?

When all is said and done, you need to take control of your life if you want to see real improvements. You cannot expect different results if you are not bold enough to make drastic changes. And the time for those changes is now!

Progress may be slow at first, but you will never regret the decision to change yourself for the better. Every step, no matter how small, is a step forward, and can thus rightly be viewed as progress. The universe has a way of rewarding the good in us and helping us to find the good in others.

By now, you should have realized that the secret to healing ourselves of the unimaginable emotional pain associated with the loss of a child, and successfully navigating through the catastrophe of life, lies in our hands.

Unless we acknowledge our own faults, and actively work to try and improve on them, our lives will never get any better.

"As human beings, our greatness lies not so much in being able to remake the world - that is the myth of the atomic age - as in being able to remake ourselves." — Mahatma Gandhi

~ 9 ~

EMOTIONAL INTELLIGENCE

Over the last decade, the idea of emotional intelligence, or EQ, has become more popular throughout the world. Unfortunately, not many people understand what EQ the term is about or why it has become so popular over the last several years. Many scientific studies have been conducted over the years and have discovered that emotional intelligence is more important in life than the average intelligence that is measured by the IQ scale. These studies, which have been conducted by both American and European universities, have proven that the common intelligence responses account for less than 20 percent of our achievements and successes in life, while the other 80 percent depends solely on our emotional intelligence.

Everyone, from students to CEOs, is confronted by not only their own emotions but the emotions of everyone around them. How you manage these emotions has a significant impact on how other people perceive us, as well as our effectiveness to get things done. When you can increase your emotional intelligence, you can become better equipped to respond to stressful situations around you with a high degree of maturity. John Mayer, Peter Salovey, and Konstantin Vasily Peterides are renowned researchers that discovered people who have high emotional intelligence tend to become better leaders and are excellent in everything they set out to accomplish.

The first person to use the term emotional intelligence was Wayne Payne in his doctoral thesis, A Study of Emotion: Developing Emotional Intelligence. In his thesis, he compared the IQ and emotional intelligence and determined that EQ was superior because it covers a wide range of faculties and aspects of a person's behavior.

Studying your emotional intelligence will help you to understand the source and impact of your emotions better. This is important because it helps to enhance one's self-awareness. Studying your EQ will also provide you with the opportunity to understand better the behavior of others and the underlying reasons why they act the way they do. Emotionally intelligent people can harmoniously reconcile what their mind and reason tell them with the voice of their feelings and emotions.

Thanks to this skill, emotionally smart people are self-confident, self-aware, creative, and energetic. They are also much more capable of handling stress and knowing how to get along with others. They are more optimistically approaching their life and don't fear change. They are the people of success.

What is Emotional Intelligence

Emotional intelligence, or EQ, refers to one's ability to identify, understand, use, and manage emotions in a positive manner in order to enhance communication, overcome challenges, relieve stress, empathize with others and defuse conflict. The scope of emotional intelligence is extensive and covers a variety of aspects in our daily lives, like how we behave and interact with others.

When you are emotionally intelligent, you are better able to recognize your own emotional state as well as the emotional state of others. Having a clear understanding of the emotional states of those around you can help you to better relate with them, achieve greater success, form healthier relationships, and lead a more satisfying life overall.

Compared to what we know as intelligence quotient or IQ, emotional intelligence is considered more important in attaining success and happiness in both your career and your life. Your ability to read and interpret other people's signals and respond to those signals appropriately will ultimately determine how far you will go in both your personal and professional pursuits of success. Therefore, it is essential that you develop a high emotional intelligence that will help you understand, negotiate, and empathize with others.

Emotional Intelligence Researchers have determined that there are five major classes of skills that are associated with emotional intelligence.

Self-Awareness

Self-awareness is your ability to recognize your emotions and the impact that they have on not only your thoughts but your behavior as well. Through self-awareness, you will start to understand your strengths and weaknesses and is a critical part of your emotional intelligence. Having self-awareness will also help you to build your self-confidence.

Self-Regulation

Self-regulation is your ability to put impulsive behaviors and feelings under control and is another critical part of emotional intelligence. While self-management doesn't prevent you from feeling emotions, it enables you to have a say in how long a feeling lasts. Learning how to manage emotions in a healthy manner, adapting to changing circumstances, and following through on commitments are just some of the critical aspects of self-regulation. There are several techniques that you can use to keep negative emotions like anxiety, anger, and depression at bay. Some of the methods include meditation and recasting situations in a more positive light. Self-regulation involves the following attributes:

- Self-control
- Trustworthiness
- Conscientiousness
- Adaptability

• Innovation Motivation

Motivation refers to the internal process that propels you toward a goal. This category of emotional intelligence requires you to set clear goals, have a defined path for reaching your goals, and a positive attitude.

Everyone has a predisposition toward a positive or negative attitude, but with motivation, you can shift how you think to more positive orientation. Every negative thought that crosses your mind can be reframed in a positive way to help you achieve your goals. Motivation consists of the following:

• Achievement drive
• Commitment
• Initiative
• Optimism

Empathy

Empathy refers to your ability to understand the concerns, needs, and emotion of others, and it is an essential element of emotional intelligence. Empathy enables you to recognize emotional cues and group power dynamics that can help you respond to the reactions of others more appropriately. People that are empathetic excel at developing others, service orientation, leveraging diversity, and political awareness.

Social Skills

Social skills are the last category of emotional intelligence. Social skills also referred to as relationship management is the ability to develop interpersonal skills that can significantly boost your chances of having a successful career and life. Being a global economy with the ease of access to information and technical knowledge, it is essential to have people skills if you want to be able to understand, empathize, inspire, and work well in team settings.

In addition to conflict management, developing excellent social skills will allow you to:

• Influence others
• Communicate

• Build bonds

Lead Psychologists agree that IQ alone isn't sufficient for achieving happiness and success in life. According to recent studies, your IQ only accounts for around 10 to 25 percent of your success, while emotional intelligence accounts for approximately 75 percent. Other studies have revealed that those with high EQ scores tend to perform better at work, and more self-confident, and make better leaders. All these factors have led to the conclusion that EQ is important and can significantly enhance a person's productivity and personal development.

Benefits of High Emotional Intelligence Having a high level of emotional intelligence can set you apart from the crowd and help you create real opportunities. Many advantages can accrue in your life as a result of having high emotional intelligence. Fortunately, the good news is that every person who is ready and willing to increase their EQ levels, if you're willing to put the work in and practice.

In the world, there are incredibly smart, yet they aren't successful or live a fulfilled life. For example, there are brilliant in academics, but when it comes to their personal relationships, they are inept. This is because while they might have a high IQ, their emotional intelligence is low.

There are many things that emotional intelligence can help you attain, including the following. Personal Effectiveness

Emotional intelligence is regarded as a critical ingredient for your own success. It provides you with the ability to manage your affairs and those of others successfully. Emotional intelligence gives you the tools and strategies that can make you more aware of yourself and teach you how to manage your emotions, both the positive and the negative, which increases your personal effectiveness.

Thinking Skills

What makes an issue challenging to solve might not be due to its complexity, but rather the perspective that you have. Old difficulties can be solved by replacing early views with new perspectives. Emotional intelligence also helps in developing your strategic thinking capacity and your ability to inspire and motivate your team.

Professional Relationships

With higher emotional intelligence, you will be able to understand better what makes people tick. This is crucial in developing a harmonious and positive working environment and relationships. By boosting your emotional intelligence, your ability to interact with others, and communicate more effectively with others will all increase. This will, in turn, enhance your professional relationships.

Leadership Capability

Effective leadership requires that you understand and empathize with the people that you lead. Emotional intelligence provides you with strategies that are crucial in persuading, influencing, motivating, and inspiring others. The most significant determinant of success in any management or leadership style is the extent to which you understand the emotions of other people and how well you respond to them. This can significantly enhance satisfaction and create a conducive environment for stronger workplace relationships.

Physical Well-Being

Your emotional intelligence has a significant impact on your overall well-being. Stress management, which is closely related to your emotional state, gives you the unique ability to react in a positive way even when you face challenges in your life. This is incredibly important because stress can end up weakening your physical skills, lowering your immune system, and ultimately decrease your quality of life.

Mental Well-Being

The attitude and the outlook that you have on your life is shaped by emotional intelligence. If you have low EQ, you likely experience anxiety, depression, and mood swings. This will end up eroding your positivity and optimism, making your life dull and unpleasant. Your mental stability is usually at its highest when all your faculties, including your ability to understand and interpret your emotions, are working right.

Conflict Management

You can't get away from conflict. However, your ability to resolve any dispute is wholly dependent on your level of understanding of the emotions of the people involved. If you can successfully discern and empathize with the feelings and perspectives of the people in the conflict, it becomes easy to solve such situations or even prevent them from also occurring in the first place. High emotional intelligence makes us better negotiators because it gives you an insight into the desires and needs of the parties in contention. When you know the bone of contention, resolving conflict becomes much easier.

Success

Your ability to focus on a goal is a total of your internal motivators and self-confidence. Higher levels of emotional intelligence can give you self-discipline and keep us on course towards attaining your goals. In addition, emotional intelligence allows you to create a better support network, persevere with an incredible degree of resilience, and overcome setbacks that stand between you and your success. An emotionally intelligent person can delay instant gratification and focus on the long-term benefits of a course of action which boosts your chances of success.

The field of emotional intelligence is still attracting studies by different scholars, what is clear, however, is that emotions play a crucial role in enhancing the quality of both our personal and professional lives. The advancement in technology has helped us to master information, but it has not replaced our ability to learn and manage emotions.

~ 10 ~

TRIGGERS

Emotional triggers are the thoughts, feelings, and events that can evoke an automatic response. The use of the word trigger is crucial because the reaction occurs automatically without self-control. While these reactions might seem involuntary like everything else, we do, the response is a matter of choice. If you want to take control of how you respond to different circumstances, then you will need to learn how to identify your personal emotional triggers.

How to Identify Your Emotional Triggers

Until you can identify your emotional triggers correctly, they will continually rule over your emotions. Rather than letting minor aggravations make you run for the hills, you need to learn how to take charge of your feelings. You can do this by first dealing with your personal stressors.

There are different groups of stressors, including the following.

Emotional Stressors

Emotional stressors can also be considered internal stressors. These stressors include anxiety and fears, along with personality traits like suspiciousness, pessimism, and perfectionism. These kinds of stressors often distort your thinking or perceptions that you have toward others. Family Stressors This category of stressors includes financial problems, relationship problems, empty-nest syndrome, and coping with unruly adolescents. All these issues can trigger an emotional response.

Social Stressors

Social stressors can come from the interactions that you have with other members of society. They can include public speaking, dating, and parties. Just like emotional stressors, social stressors are individualized.

Change Stressors

Change stressors are ones that originate from necessary changes that happen in your life. These stressors can include moving to a new location, starting a new job, getting married, having children, and others.

Work Stressors

Work stressors are ones that occur in the workplace, which is typically full of pressure. These stressors can include an unpredictable boss, endless tasks, and tight deadlines. In addition to these above stressors, there are other categories of triggers that can affect your emotional intelligence. These can include things like the decision, disease, physical, phobic, pain, and environmental.

After looking through the stressors listed above, you can start to determine the main stressors that you deal with daily in your life. It is possible to find that some of your stressors fall into more than one category.

How to Deal with Emotional Triggers

Once you've determined the stressors in your life, you need to figure out how to deal with them one at a time. Here are some of the common strategies that people use to deal with emotional triggers.

Elimination

Some of the emotional triggers that you experience can be eliminated from your life for good. For example, if a particular community doesn't give you the peace of mind that you desire, you can decide to move to a new area and start a new life. This way, you will have eliminated the social stressors entirely from your life. For the workplace, you can either ask for a transfer or look for another job.

However, some of the stressors can't be easily eliminated and eliminating some of the stressors could end up causing significant loss in your life. To deal with these stressors, you'll need to work to resolve them using some of the other strategies.

Reducing the Stressors' Strength

This is a good strategy because it enables you to co-exist with others while minimizing the impact of the stressors. For example, if loud music from your neighbor is keeping you from concentrating on your tasks, you might want to consider investing in a pair of earplugs. If you feel that your morning trip to work is a stressor, because you must drive for more than two hours, you might think about using public transportation or carpooling with others from your work.

Coping

It is said that if you can't beat them, join them. For most of the stressors, you may just have to learn how to live with them, because eliminating them from your life could end up being counter-productive. You need to come up with coping techniques that will allow you to be clearheaded and calm, even when you find yourself under pressure. The sooner you can master these techniques, the better you will become, and some of the stressors will no longer be threatening as they used to.

Talking to a Friend

If you have a trusted friend, one of the best ways to deal with stressors is to approach them and communicate your feelings to them. This way, you can get encouragement, fresh ideas, and the support you need to help you overcome your emotional triggers. You need to consider the feedback you receive carefully because it comes from an independent perspective. If you can't find a person to open up to, you can also join a support group where people who are facing similar challenges meet and talk with each other. These kinds of networks have life coaches who have experience in dealing with issues around emotional triggers.

Stay Positive

Some of the emotional triggers can have a severe impact because of our perspectives. If you are determined to stay positive, it is unlikely that emotional triggers will take their toll. You may encounter situations in your life that have the potential to trigger your emotions; however, because of your focus on positivity, these situations might not succeed in turning your world upside down. As part of living a positive life, you should try as much as possible to fight off any tendencies of anxiety. Instead of focusing on the uncertainties of the future or the troubles of the past, you can choose to stay in the present and make good of the opportunities that present themselves. While each person is emotionally sensitive to a certain degree, learning how you can manage those emotions and those triggers causing them is what makes each of us different.

~ 11 ~

RESPONSIBILITIES AND
BOUNDARIES

Whatever has happened to you in your life, the bottom line is that you are ultimately responsible for your actions, reactions and choices. If you are looking for happiness and success in your personal and professional life, you must embrace this principle. When things go wrong in your life, there is always a temptation to blame others for your misfortunes, but that won't help you find happiness in your life. If anything, it will ultimately worsen the situation and will end up sinking you into further irresponsibility.

Taking responsibility for your actions, reactions and choices, and your direction in life will be the most powerful and intelligent way that you can deal with the issues you face in life. The moment you stop taking responsibility, the perspective you have in life will shift, and often, you will start to see yourself as a failure because you've allowed yourself to blame others for your problems.

When you take complete responsibility for your life, and experience control and joy despite the circumstances you can make better decisions and choices because you completely understand that you, and only you, are responsible for the outcome of your choices. Even when events happen that aren't within your control, you have the power to determine how you will react to those events. You can either make a disaster out of a situation or use the challenges in your life as a ladder to reach a higher level.

How to Take Responsibility

One of the most critical components that you need to accept is that you oversee your life, and no one else. It doesn't matter how hard you try and convince the people around you that the events currently happening in your life aren't the consequence of your actions, you will still need to go through them and face the consequences as they come.

If you want to be able to remain in control and handle the situations you face with resolve and determination, you will need to do the following.

Stop Placing Blame on Others

Whether you are by yourself or in a group with others, you need to listen to yourself as you talk. Work to eliminate blame and excuses in your speech. The more you continue to play the blame speech in your mind, the more likely you will try to shift responsibility to others.

Seriously Consider Feedback

There will be times when you won't be able to hear your voice as you speak with other people. Therefore, accepting feedback from others is critical to your emotional intelligence. Some of the people that you talk to might be observant and honest enough to tell you about your habit of shifting blame to others. If you take this kind of feedback seriously, it can help to change you and your perception of life. It is almost natural for us to dissent to feedback that doesn't favor them. The more you reject other people's observations, the more likely you will continue with your irresponsible tendencies to your own detriment.

Plan Your Life

Your life consists of the sum of all the plans, decisions, and courses of action that you take daily. By putting a plan in place on how you want your life to run, you can successfully take control of your future and eliminate the temptation of blaming others for things that you are responsible for. Your plan should be broken down into achievable goals that you can measure your progress on.

Recognizing Your Choices

You have an overall choice on how you are going to respond in any given situation. This is irrespective of the severity of the circumstances. It is possible to be locked away in prison and still maintain your mental sanity. You have the option to focus on something more positive than the situation you are currently in. This will help you free your emotions and to a more significant extent, your entire being.

How to Set Your Personal Boundaries

When you can start to understand what personal boundaries are and what defines healthy and unhealthy boundaries, it is vital that you know how to set up these boundaries. Setting personal boundaries, emotional, physical and financial, is a process that will take some time, so you need to have patience.

Consider What Your Boundaries Are

It is almost impossible for you to create and enforce personal boundaries if you don't know what they are. Take some time to consider the things that make you uncomfortable. Establish the extent to which other people can come into your life and the things they should do as they approach you. This will help you to draw clear lines that will help you to define your personal boundaries.

Verbalize Your Needs

Don't be afraid to let those around you know about the things that you need in your life. For example, if you are bothered by the noise that someone is making, you need to have the courage to clearly tell them that you want silence and that they need to step back or go somewhere else. This will send them a signal that will inform them that they are intruding on your personal space. Put Consequences in Place Just like with any boundary violation, whether physical or emotional, there needs to be a consequence that follows it. Individuals can be experimental in that they can make a minor infraction to see whether there are any consequences. If no repercussions come up, they will continue to invade your personal boundaries, and they even might try to establish a new code of behavior when they are dealing with you. You need to deliberately put consequences in place, such as discontinuing the conversation, leaving the area, or refusing to answer to help ward off those who are looking to cross your personal boundaries.

Stand Your Ground

If you are to create and maintain your personal boundaries successfully, you need to hold tight to your ideals and value system and not back off them for even a second. The moment that you make a mistake and compromise your stand, other people will be quick to swoop in and violate your boundaries.

Emotional intelligence is reflected in how you take responsibility and define your personal space. A person that has a definite value system and a set of easily identifiable boundaries is more responsible and emotionally intelligent.

~ 12 ~

RAISE YOUR EQ

The information that passes into your brain must first pass through your senses. Whenever this information is emotional or overwhelmingly stressful, your natural instincts take over, and our capacity to act is limited. To make good decisions when you are confronted with these kinds of situations, you need to learn how to balance your emotions deliberately.

Emotion is also linked strongly to your memory. If you learn to stay connected to the rational and emotional part of your brain, you will be able to expand your range of choices when responding to new events.

In addition, integrating emotional memory into the decision-making process will help to prevent you from repeating past mistakes

. Key Skills of Emotional Intelligence

If you want to improve your emotional intelligence and your ability to make decisions, then you need to understand your emotions fully and how to manage them in any situation. To enable you to do this, you need to be able to develop critical skills for managing and controlling your stress levels. These skills can be learned by anyone who is willing to apply the knowledge they've gained into their lives. To change your behavior permanently to enable you to withstand pressure, you will need to learn how to overcome stress by maintaining emotional awareness and composure.

Rapid Stress Reduction

Stress is a part of our daily lives, but when it comes at overwhelming levels, it can end up subduing the mind, as well as the body. Stress can also hinder you from communicating clearly and ultimately interferes with our ability to read a situation accurately. For you to remain focused, balanced, and in control, you need to learn different techniques for how to calm yourself down regardless of the level of stress that you are currently facing in your life. Stressbusting is one of the methods that you can use to cope well when faced with a stressful event. The following steps can help you to develop solid stress-busting skills.

Be Aware of Your Physical Response

If you want to learn to control your emotions and reduce the impact that stress has on your life, then you need to know how you physically respond to stressful events. Carefully analyze how your body feels when you are under pressure because this will help you to learn how to regulate tension when stress occurs. People have very different reactions to stress. While some might become angry or agitated when faced with a stressful situation, others will become withdrawn and depressed. If you are one who tends to become angry, you will respond well to stress-relieving events because they will quiet you down. However, if you tend to become depressed when faced with stress, pursuing activities that are stimulating will be the best thing that you can do.

Analyze the Stress-Busting Tactics that Work for You One of the best ways to quickly reduce stress levels is through the engagement of your senses. Everyone has their own way of responding to each of these sensory inputs, and the secret is in finding things that are soothing or that energize you. For example, if you are a visual person, you can surround yourself with images that are uplifting to help you fight off stress. On the other hand, if you respond better to sound, you can find a favorite piece of music that can help you relax.

Emotional Awareness

The ability to connect to your emotions is a critical part of understanding yourself. Having emotional awareness also helps you to become calm and focused, even in stressful situations. Too many people today are disconnected from their emotions because of adverse childhood experiences that taught them to shut their feelings out when faced with stressful situations. Unfortunately, while we can deny, distort, or numb our feelings, we can't eliminate them.

Whether we acknowledge our emotions or not, they still exist. When you are emotionally unaware, your ability to fully understand your needs is hindered, which will only put you at a higher risk of becoming overwhelmed in threatening situations. For you to achieve emotional intelligence, you need to reconnect with your emotions and learn to accept them. You can learn and develop your emotional awareness at any time.

Just like with any developmental process, improving your emotional knowledge needs to be a gradual process, starting with stress management, and then moving on to learning how to reconnect with your stronger emotions. This can help you change the way you experience emotions and how you ultimately respond to them.

When you can learn to master your emotions, you can ultimately master your life. It is vital that you understand the reasons why you do the things that you do because of an inner drive to change the way you feel. For example, if you want to make more money, lose weight, or buy new clothes, you are doing this because of the feeling you get when you accomplish your goals.

People who believe that losing weight will help them to become more confident, and ultimately attract love into their life, will go the extra mile to shed off unwanted pounds. Emotions are an essential part of our life. Rather than putting them off and hiding them, you need to acknowledge them and realize the truth that lies within them.

The Emotional Triad

No matter the situation that you might find yourself in, there are three main factors that will determine your feelings about the situation. Psychologists refer to these factors as the Emotional Triad, and they include the following:

Your Physiology

Every single emotion that you experience in your life is first felt in your body. For example, if you want to feel more confident, then you need to be grounded, principled, and courageous in your speech. On the other hand, if you're going to feel more passion in your life, then you should start talking and moving more rapidly. For those people who want to feel depressed, simply must frown, breathe shallowly, slump over, and stare at the ground. The bottom line is that the way you use your body will end up changing how you feel. Emotion is created by motion.

What You Focus On

Along with how you use your body, what you focus on will also determine how you feel. If you want to feel happy, you need to focus your attention on things that make you happy. By recalling more joyful moments in your past, you can create a platform and an opportunity to be happy today. When you remove all the good things and experiences in your life and focus on the negative, you will most certainly end up feeling depressed. In life, both good things and bad things are available, and it is up to you to decide what you want to focus on.

Your Language

The words that you use can change the way you feel. If you begin making statements like, "I'm exhausted," or "I'm so bored," the chances are that you will feel tired or bored. Every single word that you speak has an emotional state attached to it. Some words that you use are disempowering, while others are encouraging and up-lifting. By exercising care over your vocabulary, statements, meta-phors, and phrases, you can control and command your emotions.

The reality of the Emotional Triad is that happiness is a choice, and the same goes for anger, sadness, and frustration. There isn't anyone who can make you feel angry or happy, but rather, it depends on how you interpret every situation that you face in your life.

How to Deal with Negative Emotions

Both negative and positive emotions are a part of our lives and can't simply be wished away. However, you can decide to deal with these emotions so that you can effectively suppress the negative ones and encourage positive emotions. There are four ways in which you can deal with your negative emotions.

Avoidance

Avoidance simply means keeping away from situations that have the potential to trigger negative emotions. For example, you might avoid approaching strangers or taking risks because you fear rejection or failure. It is incredibly common for people to turn to self-medication, like alcohol food, or drugs, to ward off negative emotions, which is just another form of avoidance.

Denial

Denial is the process of disassociating yourself from the negative emotions you're feeling by using statements like, "It wasn't that bad." While you may think that it is perfectly alright for you to go into denial about your negative emotions, the approach, unfortunately, will increase those negative emotions and will continue to intensify them until you pay attention to the negative emotions.

Learning and Using Your Negative Emotions

Learning from your negative emotions and using them to your advantage is one of the methods used to deal with negative emotions. First, you need to understand that all your emotions, both negative and positive, are there to serve you.

Your daily emotions are a guideline, a support system, or a call to action. They tell you that the activity that you are participating in either works or it doesn't. The thing that you need to remember is that you are the origin of all your emotions and that you and you alone create them. You don't need a particular reason to feel a certain way, but rather it is all your choice.

The power to command your emotions lies within you. Every emotion comes from you, and you are the only one who is suited to not only handle them but subdue them as well. With continued practice, you can take advantage of your emotions and have them work for you rather than against you.

~ 13 ~

GET CONTROL

If you find that you are frequently engaging in arguments or fights with those around you, it could be a result of anger. Anger is a normal and healthy emotion; however, when it reaches chronic levels, it can end up spiraling out of control.

Having uncontrolled anger can bring about severe consequences in your life, your state of mind, your health, and your emotional intelligence. Getting insights into anger management tools and the reason behind your anger can help you learn how to keep your temper in check.

Understanding Anger

Anger, as an emotion, is neither good nor bad. It is a normal emotion and healthy to display when you have been mistreated or wronged. While the feeling of anger isn't a problem, what you do with that anger makes a ton of difference. It has the potential to not only harm you but other people as well. Many people think that when they have a hot temper, their ability to control their anger is at its lowest point. However, we have more control over our anger than we think. You can learn how to express your emotions freely without hurting other people. When you can accomplish this, you will feel much better, and your needs will be met faster. Mastering the art of anger management isn't an easy task, but the more that you can practice it, the higher the likelihood of it becoming much easier.

Anger management affects your goal achievement, your relationships, and your level of satisfaction with your life.

The Importance of Anger Management

Many people think that they have the right to vent their anger and that those around them are overly sensitive. However, anger is incredibly damaging to your relationships and will impair your judgment. Emotional outbursts have always gotten in the way of success and will always have a negative impact on how others perceive you. When your anger spirals out of control, it can even hurt your physical health. Always operating at high levels of stress and tension aren't good for your health. Scientific research has shown that having chronic anger can make you more vulnerable to heart diseases, high cholesterol, diabetes, a weakened immune system, high blood pressure, and insomnia. When you are angry, you tend to consume vast amounts of mental energy, which has the potential to crowd your thoughts. This, in turn, can make it increasingly difficult to concentrate, see the big picture, and enjoy your life. Stress, depression, and other mental conditions are typical for people who experience frequent anger. Having out of control anger can also affect how successful you are in your career.

Even though creative differences, constructive criticism, and heated debates are healthy, continually lashing out can end up alienating your friends, family, supervisors, colleagues, and clients further and can ultimately lead to an erosion of respect, and a bad reputation will follow you.

Anger can also be so dangerous that it can cause scars in people that you relate and care about, ruining relationships and friendships. When you are always angry, very few people will lose their trust of you.

Tips for Managing Your Anger

Understanding why it is so important to manage your anger and how to avoid letting it spiral out of control, you need to focus on how different strategies that will help you manage your anger. Here are a few useful and practical tips to help you get your anger under control.

Understand the Cause of Your Anger

Nothing happens to us without cause. There must be an underlying issue that makes you struggle with your anger. Most of the problems that made you angry usually stem from things that you learned when you are a small child. For example, if you grew up in a violent house, you might have picked up the idea that anger is supposed to be used as a tool of expression to get everything your way. High levels of stress and traumatic events could also be some of the underlying factors that make you susceptible to anger. Some people use anger to cover up their feelings of insecurity, vulnerability, embarrassment, shame, and hurt. This means that these people aren't truly angry, but rather connect to certain events that make them angry. Knee-jerk responses are evidence that the temper that is being expressed is nothing more than a cover-up for other feelings and needs.

Beware of Anger Triggers and Warning Signs

Every single buildup of an anger explosion is characterized by warning signs. Some of these signs are physical in nature and are manifested through your body. Anger fuels the fight or flight system in your body, and the angrier you get, the more chances your body is going to go into overdrive. The moment you take some time to study the warning signs of your body, you can start to manage your temper before it gets out of control. It is incredibly easy to point the finger at others and blame them for the circumstances around you while forgetting that the real cause of your anger is you and how you respond to stressful situations. It has very little to do with the actions of others.

Learn Effective Ways to Cool Down

There are several different techniques that you can use to help you cool down and keep your anger under control. Some of the methods include:

• Taking deep breaths and slowly breathing from your abdomen.

• Exercising helps to release pent up energy and can help you approach a situation with a cooler head.

• Take advantage of all your senses to help you calm down.

• Massage and stretch areas of tension can help your body relax and ease tension.

• Remove yourself from the situation to help you release tension and give you the space you need to reconsider your response.

Seek Professional Help

If you haven't been able to manage your anger on your own, you should seek professional help. There are therapies, programs, and classes that are specifically for people who have issues with anger management. Many other people suffer from the same problems, and together, you can help each other overcome them.

~ 14 ~

CONFLICT RESOLUTION

Every relationship has its ups and downs, and conflict is an essential component. Learning how to handle conflict rather than wishing it away is a crucial aspect of emotional intelligence. When conflict is mismanaged, the chances are high that you will cause significant harm to your relationships. However, when you learn how to handle conflict in a positive and respective manner properly, you can create opportunities for strengthening relationship bonds. Learning how to resolve disputes is vital for improving your emotional intelligence and keeping both your professional and personal relationships strong.

Understanding the Cause of Conflict

Conflict can arise because of both large and small differences between people. When people disagree over motivations, ideas, values, perceptions, or desires, they are bound to enter conflict. A conflict can be fueled by small differences, but at the center of the conflict, there is usually a more deep-seated personal need. Those needs can be anything from safety to respect and everything in between.

How to Perceive Conflict

People perceive conflict differently. Some people will do everything they can to avoid conflict because of the painful memories that are associated with them. If you previously had unhealthy relationships, your perception of conflict could be that it all ends up in disagreements. When you have conflict in relationships, it is often viewed as being demoralizing, humiliating, dangerous, and even something to be feared. If you had a childhood experience that left you feeling powerless or out of control, conflict may be traumatizing for you. If you view conflict as being dangerous, most likely your prophecy will be self-fulfilled. If you enter a conflict while feeling threatened, it can become more challenging to handle the conflict in a healthy manner. There is a high chance that you will either blow up in anger or completely shut down.

Conflict Resolution Skills

If you want to resolve a conflict successfully, then you need to start practicing two core skills. The first is the ability to reduce stress quickly, and the second is the ability to remove comfortable with your emotions so that you can react in a constructive way during arguments or perceived attacks.

Quick Stress Relief

If you want to stay balanced and focused despite the challenges in your life, then you need to improve your ability to manage and relieve stress. The moment that you fail to stay centered and in control, chances are high that you will become overwhelmed in situations of conflict, which will affect the quality of your response. If you often feel tense or tight in your body, then stress is a significant problem in your life.

Emotional Awareness

Emotional awareness helps you understand yourself and others better. If you don't know how you feel, you won't be able to resolve the conflicts in your life amicably. Conflict resolution calls for effective communication. Understanding your feelings might seem like a simple process, but many people ignore strong emotions like anger, sadness, and fear. Your connection to these feelings will determine how you ultimately handle conflict. If you are afraid of strong emotions, then your ability to resolve differences in a dispute will be impaired.

Conflict Resolution and Non-Verbal Communication

When you are amid conflict, the most critical information is exchanged non-verbally. When people become angry, the words, they use rarely convey the deep issues of their heart. To connect with your feelings, you need to learn to listen to what is being said, as well as what is being felt. This kind of listening can inform you, strengthen you, and make it a bit easier for other people to hear you.

When you are amid conflict, you need to pay close attention to the non-verbal communication that is expressed by the other person. This can help you figure out what they are really saying, which in turn allows you to respond in a manner that helps build trust and get to the root of the problem.

Emotionally intelligent people have a better chance of success in resolving conflicts because they can put themselves in the shoes of the other party.

~ 15 ~

INTERPERSONAL SKILLS

Interpersonal skills are an excellent asset for anyone who is looking to improve their emotional intelligence and growth in their career. It is what distinguishes great people from ordinary individuals. People who have excellent interpersonal skills are treated as being more emotionally intelligent and more friendly to be around. It is entirely possible to use these soft skills and use them to improve the way you communicate with others. Here are the top interpersonal skills that you need to have if you want to improve your emotional intelligence.

Verbal Communication

Verbal communication is the most used form of self-expression. We react to situations around us and communicate our emotions through the words that we speak. If you want others to understand you, then you need to ensure that your verbal communication pathway is clear. One of the easiest ways that you can develop clarity is by speaking more thoughtfully. The more thoughtful you become, the more measured your responses will be, and people will respect you for that.

Non-Verbal Communication

Non-verbal communication is often underestimated and underrated. It has a tremendous impact on your emotional intelligence because it reinforces what you are expressing verbally. It is possible to convey an emotion or respond to a conversation without saying a single word. Your body language says something about your feelings. The way you position yourself in a room, your gestures, your voice, and your posture reveal your attitude to the people around you.

Listening

Listening is a vital personal skill that enables you to interpret and respond to conversations. When your listening skills are not sufficient, messages can be easily misunderstood, which can make communication breakdown and the parties to become frustrated. Considering that excellent listening skills can enhance your productivity, boost customer satisfaction, and increase the sharing of relevant information, it is crucial that you make a substantial effort to learn this skill.

Questioning

In today's day and age, questioning has become a lost art despite it being a useful technique that helps to build listening skills. Contrary to what many believe, questioning isn't just a tool for obtaining information, but an excellent way to initiate conversation. Questioning demonstrates that you have an interest in the subject being discussed. Asking smart questions indicates that you know how to approach problems to get the answers that you need.

Problem Solving

Life is nothing more than a chain of problems that require solutions. The speed that you solve the problem isn't as important as how you solve it. In problem-solving, there is no plan that guarantees that you will succeed. The critical component of problem-solving involves being able to identify the problem, dissect the challenge to understand it fully, examine the options, and coming up with the strategy for solving the problem.

Social Awareness

Being in tune with the emotions and needs of others is an essential skill for emotional intelligence. Social awareness makes us embrace and appreciate the success of others. It also helps you identify opportunities. Being able to respond appropriately to a social situation is a clear demonstration that you are operating on a higher level of emotional intelligence.

Many people confuse emotional intelligence and intelligence quotient. When you can learn how to command your emotions, you will be able to exercise greater control over your life and ultimately unlock opportunities that would have otherwise remained hidden. High emotional intelligence is something that everyone should be working hard to obtain. This means that you shouldn't be discouraged and sidetracked, but rather, you need to continue to press on and aggressively pursue your emotional goals.

Emotional intelligence teaches and trains you how to better relate with the people around you. With the pace at which the world is quickly becoming a global village, it is more important now that you learn how to listen and interpret the information that you are gathering from those around you. By doing this, you can learn how to structure your response and communicate better with those around you. When you have higher emotional intelligence, you will ultimately find success in both your personal and professional life.

~ 16 ~

SELF-CARE

What a difference it would make if you spent time looking after yourself. If you surrounded yourself with friends and family who loved you, if you gave yourself a break every now and then, and if you told yourself, you were doing great. What if you really loved who you were, and you were satisfied with what you had? Simple: you'd be content. You'd be healthier, happier, and more fulfilled. And that feeling would emanate from you and affect everyone you interacted with. How do you get from here to there?

We need to change our thinking and the way we consider ourselves, and we also need to change the way we look after ourselves. What we eat, how we spend our time, and how we control our environment. That means not only taking care of yourself physically by grooming, feeding, and making sure that everything else is done right – but also taking care of yourself emotionally.

Self-Care Using CBT, or Cognitive Behavioral Therapy, and Mindfulness First, we start by changing the way we talk to ourselves. And this begins with mindfulness and CBT. CBT is the current favorite approach in clinical psychology, and it is going to be one of the most important tools in this book for transforming the way we view ourselves.

Where once every counsellor you went to was using psychodynamic principles to treat people, today they are all using CBT (or an integrative approach). While it's probably only a matter of time before a new school comes along and knocks CBT off the top spot, it still represents a powerful tool that many have used to quickly and cheaply improve the lives of millions. The 'quickly and cheaply' parts are also crucial as they mean that anyone can apply the principles and see immediate benefit, improving their self-esteem with no need to spend tons of money and time on counselling. Obviously if your symptoms persist you should seek professional help, but until then you can try some DIY to see if CBT is what you need to improve your self-concept.

A Brief History and Explanation Essentially, CBT is composed of two concepts – behaviorism and cognitive psychology (as the name might suggest).

Behaviorism is the old school of thought that states how we learn to associate an event with an outcome to such a degree that we can begin treating the event as the outcome. For example, in Pavlov's famous experiment using dogs, he taught his canine subjects to salivate at the sound of the bell by getting them used to hearing the bell while they ate. This applies to your self-esteem; in that you can end up having physical reactions to conditions where you're put under pressure. For example, you might find that in social situations you find yourself trembling or sweating as through your perception you've learned to associate them with leading to embarrassment or humiliation. Alternatively, you might find yourself feeling depressed or lethargic when you're attempting something new if you've failed several times in the past. Here the bad outcomes act as 'reinforcement', instructing you that your ambitions are doomed to failure. This is a learning mechanism that we've evolved which normally helps us to avoid making mistakes and which is generally adaptive in most situations. In modern society however there are times when it's misplaced and can be psychologically damaging. Behavioral therapy to cure such associations involves 'reassociation'. This would mean teaching yourself to learn that putting yourself out on a limb can lead to positive outcomes too. You might achieve this by going to lots of social settings that you know you'll enjoy, or by trying lots of new things that you think you'll be good at. You should also make sure you surround yourself with positive people who will compliment and encourage you rather than put you down. This way you will also be getting constant reinforcement that you're a worthwhile and capable person. Since behaviorism though, psychology has moved on realizing that there is a conscious aspect in many of our problems. This is the crucial contribution that CBT makes by introducing a cognitive aspect to our brain and to our anxieties. In the case of problems like low self-esteem, the cognitive aspect could be negative ruminations where you think about how everything will go wrong, negative self-talk or talking yourself out of doing things.

~ 17 ~

SILENCING THE INNER CRITIC

People with low self-esteem will often describe how they have a 'little voice' in the back of their head constantly telling them they're going to fail. Other concepts in CBT are 'over generalization', whereby you assume that because you've failed at one task you are going to fail at all tasks, and 'false hypotheses', where you incorrectly predict that you're going to fail at your tasks. We will be employing CBT techniques in order to help overcome this self-doubt.

Mindfulness CBT practitioners then have devised various methods that you can use to combat these problems. One of the most used of these is borrowed from meditation and is known as 'mindfulness'. Here people are instructed to find a quiet place and to sit down with their eyes closed. Much like in meditation they are then instructed to reflect on their inner thoughts. This doesn't mean that they should attempt to clear their minds however, instead they are instructed to merely 'watch' thoughts as they pass by without engaging in them, merely observing the content of their brains as they might watch clouds passing in the sky. This way they can identify the kinds of things they are thinking and any destructive thoughts they might be having. As people get better at this, they are supposed to be able to do it during day-to-day activities and then intervene; spotting the negative and damaging thoughts and seeing them for what they are.

Most negative ruminations are illogical and even if they aren't they certainly do more harm than good, so learning to spot them and then put an end to them is a valuable skill. Similarly, to aid in this culture of mindfulness, people are asked to keep diaries of their thoughts and activities – then to read them back and see how anything they've said or done could be disruptive to their self-image.

Positive Self-Talk

You can also counter these negative thoughts with positive ones, utilizing 'positive self-talk' to reaffirm your worth. Here you should make sure to focus on your good point, and to remember compliments you may have received in the past. Instead of telling yourself you're fat constantly, replace this with reminders about your nice eyes or straight teeth. You'd be surprised by how affective this can be.

Hypothesis Testing

People are also told to practice 'Hypothesis testing', where they are encouraged to test their false hypotheses hopefully realizing that they are unfounded. For example, if a person is scared to speak in public because they are concerned, they'll stutter and fail, then they are encouraged to try speaking in public to find out if this is in fact the case. Often, they'll find it isn't. This also works to prevent over generalization and again to counter any negative associations they've developed. So, if you're suffering from low self-esteem then you might want to try applying these principles to your life. Make sure you continue to go out and to challenge yourself, even if you genuinely are less than skilled at what it is you want to achieve this is the only way you are going to improve. Becoming reclusive will only give you more time to ruminate and send you into a downward spiral. Similarly, surround yourself with positive friends and colleagues and try to focus on the good aspects of what you do. Support yourself with positive self-talk and try to catch yourself having negative thoughts and stamp them out. If this still doesn't work, then it's perhaps time to seek help from a professional who can talk you through the process.

~ 18 ~

SELF-FULFILLING PROPHESIES

A self-fulfilling prophecy describes a phenomenon by which what you believe to be true can become a reality by the fact that you believe it or that other people believe it. If this sounds complicated, then imagine an example. Say you're a boy at school who has an older brother who recently had the same teachers and proved very successful. By this fact alone, the other teachers and pupils will assume that this new boy will achieve great grades too. This confidence and expectation will in turn rub off on him and he'll start to see himself as someone who has great academic ability. (This is also a perfect example of how influences outside of our control can shape who we are – and why it is so important that we take matters back into our own hands!)

As you're probably aware, you tend to like things that you do well in and so by thinking you're good at academia you will then start to enjoy it more and put in more time as a result. Therefore, sports psychologists use the 'sandwich' technique when giving criticism; that's positive, negative, positive. This way they can get across their advice without damaging the esteem of the sprinter or gymnast. Therefore, you need to try and constantly increase your own self-esteem and closely control how you perceive yourself in order to increase your success.

The Law of Attraction

How you perceive yourself also speaks volumes to other people as you will reveal your self confidence in subtle ways - the way you walk, the way you speak and the way you dress and the way you act. If you act as though you deserve respect, then you'll start to believe it yourself and if you start to believe it then so will others. This goes deeper than abstract opinions however and can even be used to generate wealth and success. For example, by dressing well and wearing nice watches (knockoffs will do, no one will know) you eventually be able to afford them. If you project an image of being wealthy, then others will begin to think you're rich and successful. This can mean that your boss is more likely to give you a promotion (therefore they say you should dress for the job you want, not the job you're in). It also means others will be more likely to trust you in business and that other wealthy people will gravitate towards you (like likes like). Even the gifts you receive will be more expensive on average as you generally tend to spend more on gifts for people who own more expensive things - otherwise it won't fit with the décor, and you'll look cheap. If you act confident with the opposite sex, then they'll assume you're in high demand and as such will find you more attractive. So, dressing well can make others believe you are successful and can make you feel successful too. When I was doing my finals, I heard that many of my friends were putting on their best clothes to make themselves feel good while doing them - this was good advice but really, they should have been taking this kind of care all the time. Don't just look the part though - act the part, and over time by mimicking the actions and behavior of someone successful you'll start to pick them up as habits. Wish you spoke more clearly and slowly? They forcibly put that voice and manner on and over time you will develop it.

~ 19 ~

LOOKS

One of the biggest reasons many people suffer from low confidence is that they're unhappy with a physical feature – or indeed all their physical features. If this describes you, then you should be pleased to know that there is a lot you can do about your physical features, and there's a fair chance you're not maximizing your potential. Here's how to play the hand you're dealt and get yourself looking like a million dollars.

It's the Little Things –

How to Feel Taller

Firstly, appearance needn't necessarily mean your face, and for many men in particular low confidence can stem from not being as tall as they'd like to be. Even if this isn't a particular source of contention for you, adding a bit of extra height will automatically help you to feel more confident as you look down on people, or at least look at them at eye level, rather than constantly looking up. But it's impossible to make yourself grow taller right? Well yes and no. Basically, rather than growing taller yourself, you can make yourself appear taller by investing in insoles that increase your height. If you type into e-bay 'tall insoles', you'll find several products along the lines of what you're looking for. These only cost a small amount and can be easily slipped inside your shoe then adjusted to be taller or shorter up to around four inches. Four inches of extra height if the shoes you're wearing allow it, take you from a short-ish five nine to a tall six foot one. If you combine this with large shoes you can be rather tall. For women the same can be true of high heels, and as a bonus these also make women stand up taller and improve their gait and stride – you can't shuffle in heels.

For men bulking up will also make you more imposing and as you generally fill up more space, you'll feel more commanding and confident. Try eating large amounts of protein along with regular exercise and work on your chest and shoulders to create an imposing silhouette. It's hard to feel insecure when you're over six foot and covered in muscle. At the same time men who are conscious about their weight should make sure to do a lot of cardio and avoid fatty foods to get themselves feeling leaner and less chubby – perhaps you need to take up less space. Likewise, for women, toning your abs and tightening your behind can make you feel sexier and again improve your silhouette. To help you along the way you can always use underwear that holds in the fatter areas and plumps out the bits that need plumping. Girdles and corsets are the best known, but you can also get pants that support your bottom. Girdles also exist for guys and while it may be a bit embarrassing, they can at the same time make you feel more confident when you're out and about – no one need know!

How to Beam

You know what also makes a huge difference to the way you feel though? Posture. In the last section, we saw the power of feeling taller or bigger. This can make you physically take up more space, which in turn can drastically increase confidence. But simply by pulling your shoulders back and holding your chin up, you can have a very similar effect. Not only that, but this has a physiological impact on your mood, which helps you to feel more positive and

Putting Your Best Face On

Inserting additional lifts into your shoes might all be a bit extreme though, and if it's just your facial features you're concerned about there's still a lot you can achieve without resorting to surgery. Firstly, make sure you get a haircut somewhere nice and one that fits the shape of your head. The squarer your jaw the more rounded a cut you'll need and vice versa as a rule. If you're male you also need to think about facial hair, and while this is generally a fashion mistake it can sometimes really improve your looks – just look at Rowan Atkinson in Mr. Bean compared to the same guy in Blackadder. You might also want to try dying your hair to see if another color suits you better. If you're a woman you have the benefit of being able to enhance your features with make-up. This means using foundation to cover up spots and blemishes and blusher to bring a bit more color to your cheeks. Often those who are a little shy will try to dress and apply makeup minimally so as not to draw attention to themselves. However, this attempt to 'hide' in plain sight can cause all the same self-fulfilling prophecy effects that we have previously looked at. In other words, you shrink away, and people assume that you don't want to be seen. If you get professional advice on how to do your makeup you can maximize your good features and up your sex appeal even if you can't aid your natural beauty. A professional from somewhere like 'Color Me Beautiful' will tell you not only which colors suit you best, but also what your best features are. Normally, you will be told to focus on either your eyes or your lips, depending on which is your stronger feature, and then apply the heaviest amount of makeup here to draw the eyes to your assets and away from your flaws. So, if you have nice lips, you might be advised to use some bright red lipstick to make them look fuller and more inviting, while if you're strongest feature is your eyes you might be recommended to use a heavy eye shadow or eye liner to make them stand out. Generally, it's best not to go to heavy on both as you can end up looking like a porn star or as though you're just trying too hard, and while your colors should be bold, they shouldn't look as though you're wearing face paint – natural looking colors that suit your skin tone are to be advise. Prefer a more natural look? That's fine too – but that doesn't mean not using any makeup at all. It just means being more subtle, and carefully highlighting your best features.

Grooming

Both men and women should also make sure they groom properly. For women that means removing any stray facial hairs and moisturizing regularly. For men, that again means moisturizing to be rid of dead skin as well as trimming their nasal hairs and ear hairs which can be very foul if neglected. At the same time use whitening toothpastes and maybe even specific whitener to give your teeth a glow. Alternatively, a nicer set of glasses or a cool pair of sunglasses can improve your face and make you look intelligent or cool depending on your desired look. Spend a little more on the things that you use to decorate and adorn your face.

Basically, the take home message is not to give up on your looks. If you put effort into your appearance and ask friends for honest advice, you'll look better and feel better about yourself. There's nothing wrong with cutting a few corners or using a few sneaky tricks to improve the way you look and if you look good, you'll feel good. It's not even just about the way you look thanks to your grooming – it's also about the way it feels. Taking the time to look after yourself is a physical reminder that you do care about your looks (and yourself by extension). This is a chance to unwind, and the feeling of running a razor over your skin and opening those pores can be extremely cathartic – like you're letting go of the day's stresses. Why not spend a little more on a high-tech bathroom and invest in a walk-in shower, or even a hot tub? You could get yourself a steam room and turn your home into a mini spa. Spa breaks themselves also come highly recommended for both men and women. Having someone attentive to your needs, being pampered, and coming away smelling and looking great... these all make a huge difference to the way you look, feel, and present yourself!

~ 20 ~

HEALTH

One sure fire way to improve your self-esteem is by exercising. The obvious reason for this is that you'll improve your physique which will make you more attractive and more capable. You won't feel as physically threatened by other people, you'll win respect from others who are impressed by your new shape or envious even (you'll find that you become a font of knowledge for anyone who wants to do the same), you'll be better at sports and all physical activities, and you'll be more attractive to the opposite sex. Not bad right? That's not all exercise is about, however. If you train regularly, you'll soon find that it affects you in ways that you wouldn't have expected. Training your body is something you can do regularly that has a visible and practical effect. Over time you will see that you're directly controlling an aspect of yourself. Every time you go to the gym you come away a little bit better than you were before you go in and that's one productive thing you've done that day. Even more, when you're in the gym, trying to run an extra mile on the treadmill or lift an extra 10 pounds on the bench press, you're testing yourself and coming out better.

You're challenging yourself and overcoming it daily – over time you'll learn that you can do the same in any aspect of your life. Working out is a truly life affirming activity that can help you to grow both mentally and literally physically. Working out will also increase your mood, and so your self-esteem, in other ways too. The actual act of working out causes your body to release the feel-good hormone serotonin. On top of that it also leads to neurogenesis, the birth of new brain cells. In short training will lift your mood and improve your cognitive performance both immediately and over time.

Getting Started with a Fitness Regime

To begin training then you need to assess your current condition. If you're currently overweight, you need to be doing large amounts of Cardio (that's aerobic exercise such as running or sprinting) and cutting your caloric intake.

If you're currently very thin you need to do the opposite – using fewer repetitions of a heavier weight while increasing the amount of protein you eat (that's meats and dairy products). You can even take either a protein shakes or a weight gainer to supplement your diet.

Similarly, to lose weight you need to train more regularly – about five times a week, but to get stronger and larger you need to train more heavily and less often to give your muscles time to recover and build. To begin with you can train using a simple full body routine.

While 'split' routines and the like are more conducive to training when you're more advanced, to start with you need to get your body used to training. Each session should last about forty minutes, and each exercise should consist of three sets – that means you lift the weight however many times, take a rest then repeat for three sets. Once you begin to see progress start reading into the process in more detail and learn the tricks and techniques used by the pros. The most important thing though is that you find a program and then stick with it. Even if that program isn't perfect, it will bring some results simply because you're doing training. That also means it's much better to do something very simple two or three times a week, rather than being too ambitious right away. Adherence is what really matters here.

Nourishing Nutrition and Sleep

Nutrition can make a huge difference to the way you feel about yourself and to your mood in general. That's partly because your diet will impact on your looks and your energy levels, but also because it can directly influence your mood. Foods that contain vitamin C for example will improve your mood because they provide an influx of serotonin – vitamin C being used to make serotonin. Likewise, foods high in tryptophan will do the same thing. Almost any food will trigger a release of dopamine, which is a reward hormone. Conversely, if you don't eat regularly, you will have high cortisol leading to stress and anxiety. Foods high in zinc, magnesium, and vitamin D (among others) can all help to increase testosterone production, which in men and women is closely linked with enhanced mood, energy, and drive.

Conversely though, foods that are high in processed sugars can cause low level inflammation. This is modulated through the release of pro-inflammatory cytokines, which can also affect the brain. Ever wondered why you feel sad and low energy when you have a cold or stomach bug? Brain inflammation is quite possibly the answer! Simple sugars and processed foods (especially acellular carbs) can also negatively impact the 'gut microbiome'. This means that they can feed the bad bacteria that live in our guts and starve the good ones. That in turn has a big impact on mood and energy, seeing as these bacteria release numerous neurotransmitters and hormones, and play a big role in energy metabolism. Sugary foods also spike the blood with sugar and insulin, which then quickly dissipates. This results in a 'crash' where blood sugar is low, and cortisol is high again. Of course, processed, simple sugars also typically don't contain healthy nutrients (hence the term 'empty calories') which means you don't get all the hormone and mood support you get from the good stuff. So, if you want to feel good, then you need to eat well. Treat yourself yes, but do so by using fruits, vegetables, yogurts, and other healthy treats. That way, you'll feel better in the short term AND the long term.

Sleep

Sleep is just as important. Sleeping poorly will cause your physical appearance to deteriorate, as well as your mental health and your mood. Bad sleep causes bags under the eyes, bloodshot eyes, blotchy-red skin, and the deterioration of hair and nails over time. It also leads to weight gain. In the short term, poor sleep will leave you with low energy, and will increase stress hormones like adrenaline and cortisol. You'll be wired, anxious, and fraught. The solution is to sleep longer, and to sleep better! Consider this a crucial aspect of your self-care, that will help you to look and feel your very best.

Here are some key tips to consider:

• Get at least 8 hours every night - this is non-negotiable!

• Aim to go to bed at the same time each night. Our bodies love predictability.

• Find out your own 'chronotype' by experimenting. What times work best for you to sleep and wake up?

• Take a hot shower or bath before bed

• No technology 1 hour before sleep. Read a book and try to stay calm. This is 'winding down' time. We can also use a little CBT to fall asleep faster. Instead of worrying about not getting enough sleep or trying to force yourself to sleep, instead focus on just enjoying the relaxation. The irony is that when you do this, you fall asleep much faster!

~ 21 ~

REGRETS

Regretting the past is something that we all know we shouldn't do - and that we all know is pointless - and yet we all still also tend to do it. Unfortunately, regretting mistakes is something that is largely out of our control. We are programmed you see to learn from mistakes because in the wild it would have helped us to avoid making similar mistakes in future. We regret touching fire pretty much as soon as we try it, and thus we are very unlikely to the same thing twice. But in our evolutionary history our mistakes tended to be much clearer cut and avoidable in future.

The mistakes we make today tend to be more complicated and dwelling on them tends to be less useful. Let's take that guy or girl you liked ten years ago for instance. They were giving clear hints of interest and wanted you to make a move, but you were too shy. You've moved on since then and you're happily in a new relationship, but it doesn't stop you from regretting that past mistake. Which is just a bit infuriating. Likewise, you might have made a mistake in your career once. Maybe you lost an important document which lost the company thousands, and that led to you being demoted. Or maybe you made a mistake when you shouted at your friend in haste. These are mistakes you can't 'undo' and that you knew were wrong at the time - no future victory is going to erase them, and they'll keep playing repeatedly in your head until you go mad. Or will they?

Do Regrets Fade with Time? If you're reading this, it's probably because you're struggling with some regret about your situation with your estranged adult children. If you've noticed, I don't bring them up often in this book because this book is about you. And you're probably hoping that I'm going to tell you it goes away. I wish I could, but unfortunately, I regret to say that the evidence isn't quite so clear cut. According to one study by Gilovich et al., published in Psychological Review, some regrets will heal over time, but others will be less likely to. That's because there are two types of regret: regrets of commission and regrets of omission.

Regrets of commission are regrets about things you did, while regrets of omission are regrets about things you did not do. Guess which ones we regret for the longest time? That's right – we regret the things we don't do for longer and in fact those regrets tend never to heal (though I can think of at least one example in my personal history that largely goes against that).

This seems like a clear message to 'grab life by the horns' as it were and to 'do more stuff', but again it's probably a little more complicated than that...

That Which Has Been Done... The chances you didn't take tend to be easier to rectify than those you did. 'That which has been done, cannot be undone', and yet 'that which is not done may yet be done'. In other words, if you're regretting not doing something still... then an obvious solution is to simply do it now. Pick up the phone and get talking to the one that got away! It may not be that easy if your estranged children are not speaking to you or have blocked you or even threatened a restraining order. It makes me giggle a little bit imagining my 28-year-old son who is 6'4' and 350 pounds, going into court to ask a judge for a restraining order against his mommy because she calls and tells him she loves him.

The other point to consider is that the whole concept of 'paths not taken' is one that is somewhat arbitrary at best. The reason we regret the things we don't do most is no doubt because we never find out. We have an idealized version of how those things would have turned out in our heads, so we regret not living that possible reality.

Meanwhile the things we did do we got to see in the cold light of day – thus they tend to be considerably less interesting. Let's say you always wanted to move to Australia as a child. You choose not to because you are afraid, you don't have the money, you think it's unwise etc. and thus you spend the rest of your years wondering what it would have been like and regretting your decision not to. You may have done many other miraculous things your life – whether that's getting married and having children, being there to support your family or winning the Nobel Peace Prize... the problem is that you know what that was like, and it was imperfect. Thus the 'undone' things always seem more interesting.

Likewise, the mistakes you make you live through and so you decide they could never have been that bad. And what you also must realize is that it's completely required that you do turn down some of what life has to offer. Very often in order to experience one thing we must necessarily turn down something else. There are billions of options open to you every single second and yet you will always just choose one of them. That's an infinite undone-to-done ratio.

This might sound depressing – as though you'll never be happy with what you decide – and it's very much a case of 'the grass is always greener'. But what I'm saying is that the grass always seems greener on the other side. It's not, and what you've done is probably perfectly remarkable and worthwhile in its own right: you just must learn to see that.

If you can reframe the way you look at your roads 'untaken' then, you might find that you can overcome that feeling of regret. But would they fade over time as time went on even if you never managed this, or does the study prove that they will never go away? To be honest, the research seems to suggest that our regrets won't completely fade – and particularly when they're related to things we didn't do. But I have heard it put in a more palatable way, "Past mistakes were like carvings in a tree. They don't grow with the tree – they don't even get higher. Nor do they tend to fade and in fact in some cases they can get darker. However, while the marks don't change, the tree does and over time it grows to become significantly huger leaving the marks as a relative 'dot' in the bark'. In other words, the carving that once took up a big proportion of the tree is now just a tiny mark on a huge tree – just a very small part of that tree's history. Your mistakes are similar. They might not go away, but as you build on them and have more experiences you will find that you can bury them. They're a part of who you are, and you shouldn't want that any other way – however they are an increasingly insignificant part of who you are. The key is to accept them and grow anyway.

~ 22 ~

GRATITUDE AND
SELF-COMPASSION

There is a specific type of regret that is particularly hard to let go of: the kind where you blame yourself. Thus, one more powerful tip for being happier, calmer, and more fulfilled? Occasionally just cut yourself some slack. Most of us are extremely harsh on ourselves: more so than we ever would be with anyone else. We expect too much, and we don't allow for simple mistakes or slips. In short: we demand perfection, and we rarely give ourselves a break. When was the last time you said something, you wished you hadn't, or you didn't finish as much work as you wanted to? And how did you spend the rest of that day? Most likely, you spent it regretting your shortcomings and feeling stressed. Perhaps you let it eat at your self-esteem, or you felt you didn't deserve nice things. Even if it was just cheating on your diet, you may have beaten yourself up something rotten! Now ask yourself: how would you have reacted had someone else told you those same things? You'd no doubt have given them a break and been kind to them. So how about you be the same with yourself? This is another example of mindfulness – of being mindful of the kinds of things you are thinking, and how those things affect your mind and your mood. Are your thoughts healthy? Or are they quite damaging? One way to change your thoughts from a CBT perspective, is to try using mantras. Combine this with post-it-notes around your home that contain those notes in order to improve your mood and remind yourself to think more positively. For this to work well, those notes should be things that you already believe are true to some extent. So, if you feel that you are intelligent, then write a note reminding yourself of that. And if you feel that you have an attractive ass... write that down too and stick it in your bathroom! One more very important reminder that you should write in capital letters and place where you will see it the first moment you wake up? BE KIND TO YOURSELF Journaling can help to. Write down three things you did well today, and any compliments that people gave you. You can then read these back from time to time! This has a huge impact, seeing as for most of us, an insult has a much bigger impact on our self-image than a compliment. This practice forces you to skew that balance. Loving Kindness Meditation and Gratitude You can also practice being kinder to yourself with something called 'loving kindness meditation'. This is a form of meditation that involves spending time cultivating a feeling of kindness toward yourself. Bask in that feeling, and let it really sink in. Focus on this sensation and try to maintain it for 10 minutes at a time, a few times a week. It's truly transformative in the way you see the world. Finally, consider cultivating a gratitude attitude. This means focusing on the things you have, and the things you are happy with. This not only makes you more positive, but it brings you into the present moment and helps you to feel better about the things that you have accomplished already. It's a perfect way to combat those feelings of regret! In that journal, you should also write down 3 things that you are grateful for at the end of every day. This will force you to reflect on how much has gone right and how much is good in your life.

~ 23 ~

SOCIAL ANXIETY

Social anxiety cripples the lives of many people and can make it impossible for them to speak in public or even interact with others in large social settings. While some people experience it to this kind of devastating effect, many more find they have social anxiety to a lesser degree which can make them feel unconfident in the workplace or among friends. It can then prevent them from fulfilling their potential in their careers or in their love lives. Often social anxiety comes down to a feeling that they are somehow inadequate or that what they say isn't worth as much as what others say. People opt not to speak because they worry that what they say will be 'stupid'. At the same time, they worry that they might stutter or stumble over their words and so not get their point across properly. That people will figure out that they're nervous and get bored waiting for them to t-t-t-t-talk... One quick and easy way to improve the clarity of your speech as well as your vocabulary is to talk more slowly. The slower you talk the more time you'll have to think about the next thing you're about to say. It will also help you to project your voice more and you'll instantly sound clearer, deeper and more confident. Use CBT and Become Socially Bullet-proof However, if you're in your own head and worrying about stuttering then you'll find this hard to do as you naturally speak more quickly when you're nervous. Ironically, it's worrying about getting a stutter that will give you a stutter. So how do you get out of your own head enough to slow down and speak more confidently? There is a technique known as 'hypothesis testing'. Here you test the results of doing whatever it is you're anxious about in the hope that you find your concerns are unfounded. Interestingly though, it may be more useful if you find that you do say something stupid or stutter outrageously. The reason for that is that you'll this way test the worst-case scenario and learn in the process that there's nothing to be worried about. When teaching gymnasts to backflip on a crash mat, teachers get them to purposefully land badly on their neck or back in order to teach them that they will be okay and eliminate the fear (because again, it's being worried about backflipping that will make you pull out and hurt yourself mid-way). One way you can test this is with strangers. Strike up conversation in a shop, bar or a coffee shop and don't worry at all about what you say or how you say it. In fact, try talking as strangely as possible about as dull a subject as possible. You'll never see them again, so it doesn't matter and it's just an experiment. What you'll find though, is that they treat you just as anyone else. Politely and without drawing attention to your faults. That's human nature. You see everyone is too busy worrying about how others see them to be able to judge everyone else. You see they are worried about how you'll react to what they say. If you needed any more proof that you're just as valuable and valid a human being as they are – there it is.

~ 24 ~

ENVIRONMENT

Changing your environment can impact on your mindset in a multitude of ways and by tapping into this, you can make yourself happier and healthier. Here's one amazing example of how changing your environment can lead to a happier you: awe and wonder. Imagine being primitive man and reaching the summit of a mountain. Imagine seeing valleys stretch out for miles in front of you, and you having never seen anything like it. This sheer scope and incredibly beauty would leave you basking in awe and wonder. What's happening is that you are being forced to reconsider your place in the world – and that in turn is resulting in large amounts of literal rewiring in your brain. This process occurs alongside a cascade of hormones and neurotransmitters, which lead to the feeling of spiritual nourishment we are all familiar with. When was the last time you saw something truly remarkable that changed your perspective? Whether it's looking through a telescope or going for a hike, try to find moments of awe. It could make your problems seem suddenly very small.

Going on vacation or any trip and changing your environment can also help you to overcome habits – as our environment contains triggers that make habits hard to kick. The Healing Power of Nature Another amazing way that the environment can change your feelings is by spending time in nature. This is where we evolved, and a lush natural environment once signaled an abundance of food and resources. Thus, going for a walk-in nature can have a similar effect on us now – triggering a reduced heartrate and sense of calm. In fact, many great thinkers claim that going for "nature walks" was what helped them to come up with their best ideas. Why? Because we are more creative when we are relaxed! Your Home Finally, don't underestimate the negative impact that a disorganized and untidy home can have on your mental state. If you can tidy and organize the space around you, then you can trigger huge changes in your mood, efficiency, and more. Keeping things just a little more minimal is one of the best ways to do this, and that often means reducing clutter. This also means removing the things that you don't absolutely love – that don't bring you the most joy – which means the remainder will be only the things that create very positive emotions. While you should cut down then, you should also improve quality. We've already discussed how investing in a better bathroom can help you to take better care of yourself. The same is true of your living room, where a plush couch can make a world of difference. And it's true of your bedroom, where a beautiful picture can make you feel wonderful. Money doesn't buy happiness but treating yourself to lasting items that surround you and make you feel amazing is one way to lift your spirits every single day!

~ 25 ~

SELF-ESTEEM

I know a lot of people who have almost non-existent self-esteem, which I find both upsetting and difficult to understand. I've been practicing and sharing these self-care tips for years! Let me tell you, it's certainly better than wallowing in self-loathing. The thing is as well that these people have so much going for them that it defies all logic. So rather than wishing you were more like someone, your time would be much better spent working towards becoming more like them in that area. You can pick the best assets of every person you admire and mimic them, and once you've learned those skills, you'll appreciate them far more. Want to be in peak physical condition? Get a gym membership. Want to be more charismatic? Spend more time with other people and develop your posture and conversational style. See these setbacks not as something to get upset about, but as challenges. Imagine you're in the film Rocky – a montage starts, and you train until you're great at the things you want to be great at. I used to wish I could trade my life with celebrities who'd already found success and love – but the thrill is all in the chase. You're a work in progress and if you work your way up to the top you can enjoy it properly with the sense of perspective that it required to get there. The minute you start working towards a goal like this you have purpose and a goal and you're not a 'nobody' anymore. You're a work in progress with grand dreams... So there truly is no 'need' to be unhappy with yourself. If you're unhappy with an aspect of yourself, then change it. The thing is, no one knows what the point of life is, so how can anyone tell you you're not doing it right? Someone who's earned no money might consider themselves a failure, but if they have lots of friends and family and have led a full life then who can tell them that? So long as you pursue what you enjoy it doesn't matter if you're 'successful'. Furthermore, no one should judge anyone else on their behavior because they can't really know what's going on in that person's life. If you're acting unusual perhaps you have good motivation too? Perhaps there is method to your madness? Or perhaps you're experiencing trouble in your personal life. The real point is not to defer to the approval of others and not to let it control you. Only you can judge the value of what you do. Follow your own beliefs in your own way and you will be successful in your own eyes.

Your Blueprint for Self-Care That's the theory. Hopefully along the way you have learned about the importance of self-care and self-love, and perhaps what has led to low self-esteem and stress in the first place. But now it's time to take that theory and turn it into something practical. From all we've learned, here is your blueprint to a happier and more fulfilled you:

• Use mindfulness to better understand your self-talk

• Place mantras around the home reminding yourself of your best qualities and to 'be kind' to yourself

• Look after your appearance – spend time, money, and effort on your looks

• Try loving kindness meditation

• Look after your health by exercising regularly in a way that is light and sustainable

• Dress well

• Have a grooming regime and enjoy the process as much as the outcome!

• Get 8 hours of GOOD sleep every night

• Eat nutritious food, including

• Spend time with people you love, (and who love you in return),

• Clear and tidy your home

• Go on vacation, seek out moments of awe and wonder

• Surround yourself with beautiful items that you love

• Keep a journal and use it to write things that you are grateful for, and things you have done well/people have said about you that are flattering Take all these steps every day, and you will be sure to enjoy feelings of self-love and contentment. Everything good will grow from thereEach one of us has probably found ourselves stuck at some point. Whether we are stuck in a dead-end job or stuck in a relationship that doesn't serve us or contribute to our personal growth, it can come as a surprise to realize one day that we aren't happy.

When we aren't happy, that is a huge red flag. It means that we are not serving our purpose. We are each born with special talents, passions, and interests that can help to move our lives in a plentiful direction, and sometimes even positively impact the world around us. When we aren't being true to that purpose, we find ourselves unhappy and lacking in energy, just treating each new day as a monotonous drudging routine.

~ 26 ~

DESTINY

A lot of people might wonder what the point is. Why try to get yourself all excited to be a great version of yourself and start acting like one of those annoying over-achievers you see on infomercials who are always trying to sell you something? Isn't it just a big waste of time and energy, when we ultimately tend to stay stuck on the same track no matter what we try.

Well, sure, someone who is stubbornly bound to that way of thinking will most certainly find it difficult to progress and move forward with self-improvement, but for those of us who are dedicated to the art of mastering our destiny, there is a lot in it for us!

Life seems designed at times to bring us down and keep us oppressed. Even our own bodies seem out to get us at times; creating patterns in our neural pathways that make us hard-wired to accept defeat and stay stuck in bad habits. What many of us don't seem to realize is that becoming the best version of yourself isn't some simple tasks that can be accomplished overnight with the right mantra. It is a life-altering event that will alter the course of our future and make us rethink the past, providing us with all the insight we need into creating the life we've always imagined!

But why should we try to take the effort out of our already hectic and demanding day to chart a course toward the stars, especially when it seems that no matter how hard we try to better ourselves, we come up short? Isn't there some comfort in clinging to the chaos theory, and believing that we are floating about in life and will end up where we need to be without too much effort on our part?

Sure, maybe for some that type of mindset can be helpful, but for others, it is a trap. When we allow ourselves to be swept away in a fate that we believe we have no hand in, we give away our power and allow the suffocating world of consequence to take the reins in forging our destiny. Why should we allow the consequences of other people's choices to affect us so deeply when we could be making our own choices that will help us move toward the greatest possible good.

~ 27 ~

WHAT WORKS, WHAT DOESN'T

There are a lot of ways that we can start to take our power back into our own hands and begin to make our dreams a reality. However, that can't happen unless we are able to examine the way we are approaching life with honesty and a healthy dose of reality. When we can see ourselves honestly and accept feedback from others without taking offense, that is when we truly begin to thrive.

Mastering your destiny isn't something that happens overnight. It can take weeks, months, and years of devoted practice and discipline before you begin to see results. But that is exactly what sets apart successful people from everybody else. They are willing to look at their life and dissect their long-term goals so that they know that every day they are working toward building their empire.

The best way to begin following that same mindset is to do a little bit of self-examination. If you aren't sure what makes you tick, it is going to be a lot harder for you to get started and make significant progress. When we don't know ourselves thoroughly it can get in our way, and we may find that we sabotage our own efforts without even realizing it.

Before you even consider taking the first step toward mastering your destiny, make sure that you understand what works for you and what doesn't work for you. If you don't identify the things about yourself that help you to stay motivated and the things that you find discouraging, you are never going to be able to make progress because you will not know yourself well enough to create any lasting change.

To identify what works for you and what doesn't, you are going to need to ask yourself a series of important questions. For example, what do you find most motivating? Who inspires you to achieve your goals? Are there inspirational quotes or songs that help you to stay motivated? What types of setbacks do you find the most demotivating? What do you usually do in the face of a setback? What could you do differently? Do you have a strong support network? Does it help you more to share your plans with others or keep them secret? How and where do you work the best, and under what conditions do you find yourself achieving the most favorable results?

Being able to answer questions like these will provide you with an amazing opportunity to self-reflect and create an environment that will make it easier than ever before to master your destiny. If you don't believe you can do it and you are getting in your own way all the time without even realizing it, you are likely self-sabotaging. Whether you believe you can, or you cannot, you are correct.

~ 28 ~

STARTING NOW!

Maybe you are in another school of thought entirely than those out there who think that moving forward in life is a waste of effort. Maybe instead, you believe that you have what it takes to get your plans off the ground and truly thrive. The longer we wait to take the steps that need taken in order to improve our lives and become the perfect versions of ourselves, the less motivation we will have to follow through. The only way that we can truly become the masters of our own domain is by taking the steps that need taken *now*.

Procrastinating never helped anybody. The only way to achieve a lofty goal is to have a plan of action, and to be willing to follow through on that plan. When we don't, we are basically feeding ourselves to the wolves. Without discipline and a strong devotion to achieving our goals and dreams, then we are essentially wasting our own time! That is the least productive thing that we can be doing when what we should be focusing on is mastering our destiny!

Starting now, make a promise to yourself that you are no longer going to make excuses to yourself about why it is that you can't seem to make your plans work out in your own favor. Stop telling yourself that you are going to follow your dreams later and take that first step toward realizing your full potential!

Each one of us experience obstacles when it comes to being true to ourselves and our visions. Life wasn't set up to cater to us and provide us with the time and resources that we need in order to make ourselves happy. Our happiness is in our own hands, and it is up to us to ensure that we are doing everything in our power to see to it that we achieve our potential. When we are allowing ourselves to be washed away in the chaos of every-day life, we are not doing what it takes to become the best versions of ourselves. Instead, we are bowing our heads and giving our power away to the circumstances that are beyond our control.

But we all have control! All of us have a unique purpose in life, and talents and interests that make us who we are truly meant to be.

So, while it may seem discouraging at times to try to move forward in life when it seems that the odds are stacked against you, never forget that you have the power to be the best version of yourself! You call the shots, and you can learn to structure your life and make choices that will benefit you now and for years to come.

You will learn everything you need to know about taking control of your own destiny and paving the way to a future that is both fulfilling and exciting. Life is never better than when we are inspired and passionate, working toward goals and dreams that most people let pass them by. You don't have to be one of those people any longer.

It has never been easier to take your power into your own hands and create the future of your dreams. By following the blueprint outlined for you, you will leave no stone unturned in providing yourself with the tools and inspiration to make your dreams into a reality. The only person who is left standing in your way is you, and all you must do to get there is to take that first step.

So, stop surrendering control of your fate to the chaos around you and begin to move forward into the life you have always envisioned for yourself. Not only is it better for you, but it is better for the world at large. When we are working toward our purpose, it is inspirational and tends to have a ripple effect on those around us.

Be that beam of light in another person's dreary day. Show the world that mastering your destiny truly is possible! Not only is it crucial to your own happiness, and the betterment of human society, but it is what you *deserve*. So go for it! Don't waste any more time. Become the master of your destiny, start today!!!

~ 29 ~

ADVERSITY

Experience is the best teacher; adversity is the most accomplished trainer. As I always say, everything is either a blessing or a lesson, and if we learn from that lesson then it too is a blessing. I call it a "Blesson".

No one ever wants to face misfortune and loss, especially a loss like we are experiencing. We would all have preferred to go through life, enjoying the ride without bumps. However, things are not always as planned and life is not a bed of roses and chocolates, there are always thorns somewhere. Tough times are unavoidable in all aspects of life. The truth that many people wish were not true, but is, is that adversity is inevitable. There're no magic potions or wands that can make an individual avoid troubles and misfortunes in life. Therefore, you shouldn't be hoping that you won't encounter unpleasant periods in your life. Rather, you should be hoping that you won't experience difficulties that will break you to the extent that you won't be able to rise. Indeed, there are terrible situations that can shake a person and make you feel you are cursed. However, if you keep rising from the ashes like the phoenix, you can live a beautiful life.

Adversity isn't avoidable. We face challenges and sad days because we have dreams and aspirations we want to accomplish. So, we become frustrated when we don't achieve them. If you have goals you want to achieve, adversity is inevitable.

We too all have loved ones and things we want to work out. We all hope to enjoy the companionship and camaraderie of our friends and families, especially our children, for a long time. However, we now know this too often is not the case. Sometimes, we lose them to unfortunate situations such as diseases and accidents. Even worse is when those situations are intentional. Those days are sad and dark in our lives. It is often tough to move on after the loss of a person very dear to us. Sadly, these situations are part and parcel of life. So, adversity isn't avoidable because we don't have control over situations such as how long our loved ones will live and/or love us back. We care about them and will be devastated when we lose them.

One of the biggest differences between human beings and robots is the fact that we have emotions, but they don't. Our feelings are some of the most beautiful parts of our lives. They are the reason we feel appreciated when people celebrate us on our birthdays or when we achieve something significant. Our emotions are also the reasons we feel connected to loved ones and enjoy spending time with them. However, our feelings are also responsible for unpleasant states such as depression, anxiety, and suicidal ideations. It is because you can feel that you are sad when you experience heartbreak. A robot, regardless of its sophistication, doesn't understand such things. Your feelings are also responsible for experiences such as betrayals, disappointments, and frustrations. You will always have reasons for such feelings if you are alive. Therefore, adversity isn't avoidable.

In the words of Booker T. Washington, "Success is to be measured not so much by the position that one has reached in life as by the obstacles which he has overcome." You should not ignore such wise words. Having been a leading voice of former slaves and their descendants who weathered oppression at different times,

Washington knows a thing or two about adversity. So, you should listen to what he has to say. You might not like the sound of it, but adversity is necessary. It is that trainer that takes you by the hand and leads you to the destination of your success. So, find comfort in those days when it feels as though the universe has a grudge against you. It is a training that will take away the dross from your silver and make you a shiny star. According to Tony Robbins, "Problems are the gifts that make us dig out and figure out who we are, what we're made for, and what we're responsible to give back to life'. So, quit cursing your luck during those moments you feel like your world is crashing. Your training is on! If you see things this way, you will be able to build more resilience. There is no other way to make a person strong and rugged than the tough times he or she has had. Those moments make you realize that you are stronger than you think.

When you are always avoiding challenging situations, you are missing the opportunities to train yourself for future challenges. Below are the reasons you should not run away from challenges.

You'll Not Be Able to Achieve Your Goals

There are always challenges you must overcome before you can achieve a goal. Indeed, the level of difficulties differs. However, you must encounter and overcome difficult situations to accomplish your dreams and aspirations in life. Therefore, it isn't surprising that Booker T. Washington said earlier that the success of a man should be measured by how many obstacles he has overcome. No one can become a success without solving problems. Anyone who is not willing to succeed despite odds stacking up against him should forget about becoming an achiever.

You'll Become Vulnerable

The last thing you want is to be treated like a weakling. Nonetheless, you can set yourself up to be vulnerable to changes when you have a culture of looking for the easy way out. This approach will make you restricted to your plan A. You will not be able to recover once something interferes with your original plan. For example, you will not be able to come up with another winning strategy as an entrepreneur once your initial strategy isn't working.

You'll Not Be Able to Cope Effectively with Stress

Whether we like it or not, we cannot avoid stress. Therefore, it is crucial that we have excellent coping mechanisms and strategies to avoid being overwhelmed by stress. When you have faced a stressful situation before, you won't be anxious when facing it again. However, when you are new to a situation, you might not have the confidence to face it because you are naïve. This state of mind makes you prone to mistakes, which can be costly and damaging in some situations.

It's easy to fall for the deception that some people are naturally more resilient than others. The truth is that resilience can be learned. You can be more sturdy and rugged when you understand some crucial facts about turbulent times. This chapter will explore some vital things you need to know about adversity that can give you a paradigm shift when facing difficult situations.

Tough Times Don't Last Forever

You've probably heard people make this statement many times such that it is beginning to sound like a cliché. You just must accept the fact that it is an evergreen fact you need to keep remembering repeatedly to scale through the hurdles and challenges of life. The reason two people face the same challenge but have different responses is their state of mind. The truth is that there are people around the world who have faced more difficult situations and still succeeded where you failed. So, you will be doing yourself a lot of good by choosing not to give excuses but finding solutions to the problems you encounter. The first thing you need to realize about turbulent times is that they are, most often, short-lived. The intensity and circumstances surrounding some situations might make you feel that you have come to the end of the road. Nonetheless, it's nothing but a mirage. If you choose to be calm, you will find a way out of the problem. Tough times are only for a while. The following facts confirm this claim:

You Have Been in Trouble Before

When you realize that you have had challenging periods in your life in the past and you pulled through, it should make you know that troubles are only for a while. They come and try to throw you off balance. However, if you can stand your ground, you'll only get stronger.

You Had Felt All Hope Was Lost in The Past

Another reason you shouldn't lose hope in the current situation is that you had been in seemingly hopeless situations before, and you survived. If you could survive back then, why can't you repeat the feat again? The current situation is another challenging circumstance trying to break you. Just like previous times, there is a way out this time around. Nothing lasts forever, including your troubles. You need to remember that statement whenever you are experiencing tough times that might ruin all the progress you have made recently.

Adversity Is for All

One of the reasons people struggle to recover from turbulent times is that they feel that life has been more unfair to them than others. It's easy to compare yourself with other people in the modern world, thanks to social media. However, what you might be forgetting is the fact that people often post their best moments online. They hardly post pictures or say anything about the days they are broken because of an unpleasant situation. So, you feel bad and worthless because you feel life has dealt you unfair cards while favoring others. However, it's not true that some people are handpicked for suffering, while others are selected for positive experiences. Life is like a coin: it has two sides. One side of it is full of pleasant moments, while the other side is full of disappointments and frustrations. Therefore, don't get too excited when you are experiencing the side of the coin that is full of enjoyable situations and think that is what you would always get from life. You should keep the memories safe because you will need them during the days when things turn awry for you. In the same way, when life has flipped to the other side of the coin where there's adversity, don't think that is the end of your life. If you keep calm and forge ahead, you will soon see the light at the end of the tunnel. The beautiful thing about life is that it is fair to all. How? We all experience its two sides. Besides, no one is allowed to choose the part of life they want. Not even the richest men and women can choose what they want in life. Indeed, their money can take them to a great extent. Nonetheless, there are limitations. If money can save everyone, rich people would never die of any sickness. However, famous and wealthy people lose their lives while receiving treatment. Besides, they also lose their loved ones. They experience divorce and heart-breaks, just like any other person. For example, Andy Murray, a popular Tennis star, lost his former girlfriend due to his habit of playing games a lot. So, don't think you lost your relationship because you're broke. Whoever loves you will stick by you regardless of your financial capability. Regardless of your fame, money, and social status, you will have both sunny and rainy days. Enjoy your beautiful moments and share them with the people that matter to you. Nonetheless, on those days when it's as though life isn't smiling at you, remember that adversity happens to all.

There's No Glory Without Adversity

Finally, it's crucial to remember that you cannot become a champion without tough times. Conquerors are what they are because they are battle-hardened. They have been hit at different times, but they refused to give up. The best military units in the world were forged in the furnace of adversity. They have been physically and mentally trained to be alert and respond to problematic situations. Champions don't see challenges and break down in tears. Instead, they eat trouble for breakfast. When you see how calm some people are when facing turbulent times, you might be tempted to wonder if they are human beings. However, nobody was born that way. We become weak or strong due to our previous responses to challenging situations. When you run away from a problem, you will have to keep running from similar situations for the rest of your life. However, when you confront the problem and solve it, you'll not be anxious when you are in similar situations in the future. If you keep running away from challenges, you will remain mediocre for the rest of your life. You will have to endure watching others enjoy the limelight because of their grit and determination. You'll always be in the crowd celebrating others, but you'll never be celebrated. The world doesn't award or celebrate people who break down when they are facing difficult situations. Rather, the world celebrates people who refused to give up even when the odds were stacked against them. The stories of such people are the inspiring biographies and autobiographies we read today. Their stories are made into blockbuster movies so that others facing similar situations can learn from them. The ball is in your court now. Will you give up or choose to stand up to your "Goliath" and become a champion? I implore you to choose the latter and not the former because that is the only way you can be celebrated.

Adversity happens to all. Contrary to popular opinion, famous and wealthy people also experience turbulent times that could have derailed their upward trajectory.

Walt Disney, the man who gave us Tom & Jerry and other classic animations is known all over the world for his creativity and ability to create thrilling cartoons. However, many people are not aware of the story behind his success. Do you know that he was once fired from the Kansas City Star? Why? His editor felt that he lacked the creativity and ideas needed to succeed at the top! Of course, it sounds ridiculous. However, this is the truth. If you think that this story is shocking, you need to wait until you hear more about this great man. Undeterred by his termination, he formed his first animation company in 1921 in Kansas City. He would ship his cartoons to a distribution company in New York and get paid six months later! Apparently, no company can survive on such a ridiculous arrangement. He eventually closed the firm because he could not afford his rent and could barely feed himself. You are wondering how a man who encountered such challenges became nominated for 59 Academy Awards eventually? He knew within him that tough times don't last forever and refused to give in even when the odds were stacked against him.

Oprah Winfrey is the self-made billionaire. Her story is an inspiration to many people around the world today because she is an example of how adversity can make us stronger. She had many reasons to give up and believe that she wasn't destined for the top. However, she didn't give up and kept forging ahead. She was born into a working-class family where poverty was the order of the day. Her mother gave birth to her while she was still in her teens. Unfortunately, Winfrey became pregnant when she was fourteen and gave birth to a child who died shortly after birth. It sounds all gloomy, and it was as if her life would only end in doom. Nonetheless, she had different ideas. She would go to school and became a journalist. Things didn't get better immediately despite her commendable efforts to improve her life. In one of her first jobs, the producer advised her to quit because she wasn't cut out for television. However, she didn't allow those negative words get to her. She kept pushing, and she has inspired many people around the world because of her sheer courage and determination to succeed.

Bill Gates is one of the wealthiest men in the world. However, the poster boy of Microsoft wasn't always a success. He struggled to find his niche in the early part of his life before he eventually got it right. Gates started Traf-O-Data, a company that was created to generate reports for roadway engineers from raw traffic data. He started the company alongside two other businessmen. Nonetheless, things didn't go as planned and expected. They had to close the company when the machine that was built to process the data tanked upon presentation to a Seattle County traffic employee. However, Gates wasn't deterred by this unfortunate situation. He decided to start from scratch by learning the lessons from his first experience. The lessons from his first failed attempt to build a company gave him the blueprint for one of the biggest companies in the world.

The story of Colonel Sanders showed us that it's never too late to start a global brand. Indeed, it's always better to start early. However, Colonel Sanders proved to us all that you can start a thriving business even at an old age. He started building his fast-food empire when he was already sixty-two years old! Yes! You read that correctly. He was at a stage in his life when many would be enjoying their retirement or looking forward to it. Nonetheless, he decided to go against the status quo. He presented his chicken recipe to different restaurants. Reports have it that he was rejected by more than one thousand people. However, the colonel was resilient enough not to give up. His determination eventually paid off when he found success with a restaurant outside Utah. The restaurant became the first Kentucky Fried Chicken. The company tripled its sales in a year thanks to the colonel's chicken. Whenever you feel like giving up, remember the doggedness of this man and hang in there.

The brain behind the Harry Potter story is JK Rowling. A tremendous success, isn't she? However, when you find out what things were like for her before her breakthrough, you will appreciate her success more. JK Rowling had felt that she had written something so beautiful publishers would be scrambling to publish. Nonetheless, things weren't the way she expected. She would go on to submit the manuscript to twelve major publishers who all rejected it to her dismay and shock. It was a work she had produced despite encountering challenges that would have made others quit writing for something they felt would be more lucrative. She was divorced and had a child to support by the time she finished the first parts of the book. So, during those hard times when the work was rejected, she could have felt that writing wasn't her thing. Nonetheless, she decided to try again. She submitted the manuscript a year later, and Bloomsbury accepted it. The company extended a small one thousand five hundred Euros. However, it turned out to be one of the best decisions the firm ever made.

Even if you aren't a fan of horror, the name Stephen King still rings a bell. He is a fantastic example of the success we can achieve when we choose to try again after several denials. King could have given up on one of his greatest works ever, Carrie, if he had listened to the voice of critics who told him that his ideas were outlandish. He made a difference at a time when horror wasn't in vogue. His times weren't like our days when it's easier to publish books. King submitted the manuscript of Carrie to thirty publishers, but they all turned him down. Think about it again. One, two, three, four... come on! Many people would have given up already. Interestingly, one of the publishers told King to forget about publishing the book because "negative utopias" don't sell. In fact, King had given up and thrown the manuscript into a bin. However, he gave it one more trial when his wife retrieved it and encouraged him to try one more time. It sounded ridiculous. Why will the thirty-first attempt be different from the first thirty? King listened to his wife, and the rest is history.

One thing is certain; difficult periods will never leave you the same way they met you. They will either break or make you. Regardless of the support you get from the people around you, you have a vital role to play to ensure that you come out stronger and not become vulnerable after the experience. There are some benefits you will enjoy when you choose to stay strong during sad days. Here are some of them.

Greater Resilience

Resilience is the ability to bounce back after a setback. It's a virtue many people don't possess. Unfortunately for them, it's a skill that everyone must possess because of the unpredictable nature of life. The topsy-turvy nature of life where you are smiling in the morning and sad in the evening requires mental strength to stay strong in the face of adversity. Only resilient people can weather the storm and still reach their destinations. Lack of resilience is the reason people suffer from mental health disorders such as depression and anxiety. It's also the reason some people feel that the best decision they could make during dark days is to take their lives. So, it's crucial to build a resilient spirit. However, you can never achieve this feat when you have never had to weather the storm. It's adversity that trains you to be mentally strong. When you face a challenge, and you come out on the other side in flying colors, you have increased the level of your resilience. This doesn't mean that you should crave and desire to be in unpleasant situations. However, when you find yourself in one, see it as an opportunity to build the mental strength for the future.

Enhanced Problem-Solving Skills

Just like resilience, problem-solving skills aren't inherited. They are acquired as a result of facing and overcoming challenges. You cannot know how to solve a problem when you don't have the right attitude. Your attitude is your mental disposition to a particular thing or situation that triggers a specific behavioral pattern. When you have the right attitude, you will believe that every problem has a solution, even when you don't have the answers yet. That positive state of mind will inspire you to ask the right questions from the right people and eventually find ways to solve the problem. Indeed, the right mindset will take you far. It will make you dogged and rugged. However, you cannot solve a problem unless you have the skills. You need to know how to tackle a challenge, and nothing gives you that better than when you have dealt with a similar problem in the past. So, when you face a challenge and overcome it, you have enhanced your ability to solve problems. You will be able to use the experience to solve similar problems in the future. You know what to do, and that gives you an edge over others who are new to such situations.

Leadership Skills

Leaders are chosen and trusted because of their experience and ability. No one wants to hire a person who has never driven a car before to be his or her driver. You want a person you can trust to get you to your destination with minimal stress. When you have faced adversity in the past, and you stood your ground, you'll enhance your suitability as a leader. It's natural that people will want to trust you. You'll command their respect when they know that you have been through similar situations before and succeeded. Great leaders are men and women who can keep a calm head when there is a storm. They are the ones others trust as a source of inspiration when the chips are down. Everyone needs that leader that will stir up optimism during the dark days when throwing in the towels seems like the obvious choice. People always need people they can believe in. They want to believe in you. They want to be sure that you know what you are doing, even when what you are saying doesn't make sense to them. It is the days of adversity that prepares you for such a sensitive role.

Higher Self-Esteem

It's natural that you'll have a sense of accomplishment after overcoming a challenge. You'll be proud of yourself, and this improves the way you see yourself. You will see yourself as a person that deserves the respect and love of others because you can add value to their lives. When you have low self-esteem, you are likely to have low self-efficacy. Your self-efficacy is the level of confidence you have in your ability to succeed in a task before performing it. When you have low self-esteem, people will find it difficult to trust you to handle their projects, which can also take its toll on your chances of getting a job. It will also make others not want to trust you to lead them. They will see you as a person who cannot lead himself or herself so you should not talk of leading others. Low self-esteem can also affect your chances of making new friends, which can be socially damaging.

Empathy

When you have never been through what others have been through, you'll find it difficult to empathize with them. There is no level of understanding you can have that can be the same as a person who has lost his or her loved one before. If you have never had that kind of experience, you cannot have a full grasp of what such people are going through. The world is full of many destructive critics today who are either hypocrites or just lack the understanding of what others are going through. Some football pundits who have never coached any football club before are fond of making damaging remarks about current coaches. It's easy for them to judge others because they don't know what it means to try to make over twenty people do what you want while keeping them happy. When you have been through tough times, you will be able to relate well with people going through such periods of their lives. You'll not tell them to just move on from the situation. You'll have words of encouragement for them. If you are their boss, you'll not have issues with giving them days off to recover emotionally from the shock.

Lower Anxiety

Some people have a culture of being calm and collected even when they are facing extremely challenging situations. You expect them to break down and shed tears, but they seem unmoved by the problem they are facing. In most cases, such people have an experience of being in such situations in the past. They are hurt, but they know that they don't have to make decisions they will regret later due to how they feel at that moment. Such people exude confidence and transmit tranquility that is often shocking. In some cases, they are the ones that will be encouraging the people that have come to console them. This commendable and exemplary state of mind comes from facing different unpleasant situations and choosing to move one. You can also acquire this mental state when you choose to focus on the positives when going through stormy periods. Giving up or standing up is all about making a choice. When you are experiencing setbacks, the obvious choice is throwing in the towel and telling all who cares to listen about your predicaments. However, the good news is that you have another option. You can choose to look at the brighter side and forge ahead. It is never over until you say so.

~ 30 ~

DANGERS OF WITHERING UNDER PRESSURE

When you break down when facing difficult periods, you have a lot to lose. It doesn't only show that you are weak but also shows that you have not been mentally prepared for the days of adversity. Here are some of the dangers of bowing down to the pressures of life.

Depression

According to the National Network of Depression Centers, one in five Americans will be affected by depression in their lifetimes. This psychological problem, alongside anxiety, is one of the leading mental issues in the world today. This fact isn't too shocking because the modern world is full of potentially mentally damaging situations. When you are not sturdy enough to weather your stormy days, you will plunge into depression. Note that depression isn't the same as the regular brief moments of sadness we experience due to an unpleasant occurrence in our daily activities. What makes it depression is the intensity and the period. A person suffering from depression will experience intense feelings of sadness that can last for a significant part of the day. It can even last for days or weeks. One of the signs of depression is social withdrawal. This is a situation where you prefer to stay more indoors and sleep on your bed than go out with friends and family. There is nothing wrong with having occasional times when you just want to be alone. However, it is a problem if it is something you do a lot. Talk to a therapist, life coach or trusted friend, as soon as possible if you often experience negative emotions before it leads to suicidal ideations.

Lack of Self-Confidence

If you don't believe in yourself, no one will take that gamble on you. It's only in very rare cases people hand responsibilities to people who don't believe they have what it takes to succeed in a role. One of the reasons such people are given responsibilities is usually because there is no other person that can be trusted to take the role. When you allow your challenges to overwhelm you, your confidence will be shattered. You will get used to giving excuses for your failures. In fact, in most cases, you would have said it beforehand that you'll not succeed in the task. So, when you fail, you will remind your critics that you have already predicted your failure before then. It's alright to have a realistic evaluation of your abilities. Nonetheless, the truth is that there are cases you will never know what you can do until you try. So, the best test of your ability to solve a problem is to try. Some people have been lucky enough to stumble on the solution to a problem because they tried. Such people made their own luck. Luck only favors the bold. Approach a situation like someone who has nothing to lose. If you fail, you would have learned how not to do it. Loss of Trust If you want people to trust you, then you need to start facing your challenges and seeking ways to overcome them. If you have a history of petering out when the going gets tough, no one will trust you. This can be problematic and limiting when you have ambitions to attain leadership positions. One of the attributes of great leaders is their ability to solve problems. No one will remember the leader who went into hiding when things weren't going smoothly. If you want to become that person others can trust during their stormy days, you must be known for your ability to stay strong when you were facing challenging situations. You can never give what you don't have. It is when you have been able to solve your own problems that you can help others.

Fear

Fear is part and parcel of our lives as human beings. It is the reason we build strong walls and fences around our homes and communities. It is also the reason we go for medical check-ups. We don't want anything that will compromise our security or damage our health. However, it's a problem when you are overwhelmed by your fears such that they prevent you from attempting to make the best out of your life. The days of adversity trains you to face your fears and learn to overcome them. However, when you run away from challenges, you will become a slave to fear. You will be afraid of failing because you don't want people to criticize you. You don't want others to mock you. So, you end up always giving excuses for your fears. You might call it being realistic. However, that is far from the truth. If you don't know how to do something, learn about it from people who can put you through. The modern world offers countless materials that can help you learn how to do anything. So, the lack of information is no longer a tenable excuse. Don't live your life in fear. Face your challenges and damn the consequences.

Shame

You'll live the rest of your life in shame and guilt when you re-member how you backed down when you should have shown more courage. It gets worse when you see others who had more chal-lenges succeed where you had failed. You don't want your story to be that you had failed earlier in life because you were too afraid to take a bold step. You cannot afford to live the rest of your life in the shadows because you often break down when facing challenging situations.

Now is the time to build mental strength by making the best out of what life throws at you. Stop complaining about the things you cannot change and start working on the things you can improve. When life hits you, stand up and walk again. You will wish you did so later in your life. You don't have to remember your youthful days with shame and regrets when you grow older.

Suicidal Ideation

When you keep breaking down whenever you face unpleasant situations, you might end up taking your life someday. It all begins by seeing yourself as a person that doesn't deserve to be loved and treated with value. Lack of resilience will make you prone to errors of judgment because you will often blame others or circumstances for your predicaments. You'll believe that life has been fairer to others than to you. You will blame your parents for your poverty and your gene for your lack of dexterity and creativity. Indeed, your parents and other people in your life might have contributed to your lack of opportunities. For example, they might not have sponsored your education. Nonetheless, it is not an excuse. The world is full of people who educated themselves due to their determination and refusal to give excuses for failing in life. So, at the end of the day, you are responsible for whatever you make of your life. So, start taking more responsibilities today. Failure to do so can lead to having thoughts of taking your life at different points.

~ 31 ~

RESILIENCE

Now that you have a good grasp of the benefits and disadvantages of standing up during tough times, it is time to discuss how you can build a resilient spirit. The tips below will help you in this regard.

See Every Challenge as An Opportunity

The difference between people who stand strong when facing challenges and those who break down is their perception. The person withering away due to the situation feels there is no way out again. He or she feels things can never get better. Such people are fixated on what they have lost and find it difficult to imagine starting all over again after the effort they have put in initially. However, resilient people look on the bright side. They see the experience as a learning curve and are willing to start all over again. They aren't happy about the situation. Nonetheless, they know that they will be better off by forging ahead. They know that they will not gain anything by wailing and complaining. They understand that complaining and sulking will only make things worse. So, they choose to see the unpleasant experience as an opportunity to be better prepared for future incidents. Failure doesn't mean you aren't good enough. Rather, it shows that you might not have been prepared enough or the situation is just out of your control. So, if you want to build a resilient spirit, you must see setbacks as opportunities to grow and learn. You need to start seeing adversity as a trainer that has come to make you mentally stronger and better prepared for the future.

Always Learn from Your Past "

Learn from yesterday, live for today, hope for tomorrow. The important thing is not to stop questioning. Albert Einstein said, "Whoever doesn't learn from the past is not smart. Such a person is wasting valuable experiences that are supposed to make him or her better'. It might sound strange that some people don't learn from their mistakes. One of the reasons some people make the same mistakes is that they feel their past errors were just coincidental. So, they feel things will be different if they stick to their guns. Indeed, there is a place for sticking to your guns when you believe in the process. However, you should have a better and advanced version of the original approach that failed. The fact that a process didn't work out doesn't mean you need a complete overhauling. You might only need to tweak your approach a little to increase your chances of getting the right result. Just like the advice of Einstein, you cannot afford to stop growing and learning. A crucial part of your learning process is your past. Your past contains both the sweet and bitter experiences that have shown you better ways of doing things. You should leverage them to build a resilient spirit when facing challenging moments.

Reduce Your Expectations

One of the reasons people get disappointed in life is that they have heightened expectations. There's nothing wrong with having desires you hope will be met. You can expect to have a fantastic marital relationship. In the same way, you can crave your dream job. You need such desires so that you can pursue them as much as possible. However, you shouldn't see these goals as do or die affairs. In other words, if your relationship or even marriage doesn't work out as planned, remember JK Rowling. She is a good example of how a failed marriage shouldn't be the end of your life. Indeed, we cannot deny that it is a situation that can be emotionally devastating.

After all, in an ideal case, people marry because they are in love and hope to spend the rest of their lives in the loving arms of each other. So, when things go awry, it can be psychologically tasking. Nonetheless, you must move on. Believe the best about your family, spouse, job, and every other aspect of your life. However, you shouldn't expect that nothing can go wrong. No one wants something bad to happen. However, you should have it somewhere in your mind that things might not go as planned. When you have this moderate expectation, you will find it easier to recover in case things go bad.

Be Optimistic

Despite the volatile and unpredictable nature of life, we cannot do without hope. We need optimism to go through life. Optimism is a positive expectation regarding certain things. You need to be positive during the days when things are rosy and pleasant. You shouldn't be fearful that something bad will happen that will turn your world upside down even though that possibility cannot be ruled out. However, you shouldn't be making predictions of doom about any aspect of your life. This practice is tantamount to making a self-fulfilling prophecy. It is too negative, and you shouldn't engage in such limiting behavior. Moreover, the best time you need to be optimistic is after a major setback. You need to convince yourself that you can still live a happy and fulfilled life despite the unfortunate occurrence. People take their lives when they get to that point of hopelessness, where they feel that their lives aren't worth living anymore. You should guide against that. Don't just think optimistically; you should also write and speak optimism. Say it loud to yourself after a setback that you are coming back better and stronger.

Take Life One Step at A Time

You cannot afford to live your life based on the pace of the modern world. If you do so, you'll be overwhelmed with stress and pressure. You should take things slowly. When you are in a hurry to succeed, you'll struggle to recover when you face turbulent times.

You'll feel that you are wasting valuable time, and that will lead to frustration. The most important thing is that you shouldn't be stagnant. If you are making progress, regardless of how little it seems, you should be satisfied with your life. Of course, if you find ways to accelerate your progress, you should take advantage of them. However, you should avoid desperation to get to the top because it can leave you with scars that will never heal. Don't be too competitive. Avoid unnecessary comparisons with others. Focus on yourself and the progress you are making. The only reason you shouldn't be happy with yourself is when you are not making progress personally. Don't measure your success by what others have achieved. It's crucial that you take things slowly, especially after a setback. Pick up yourself, walk, and then run again.

Be Flexible

There are times you need to be rigid. You need to stick to your guns sometimes because there are many people out there who feel you cannot succeed unless you dance to their tune and use their approach. However, the truth is that there is no formula for success in life. People use different techniques to achieve a level of success in different endeavors in life. So, you should have a strategy and believe it will work. It's always better to do something the way you want it and fail rather than follow a person's recommendation and fail. The latter hurts more. So, don't allow people to throw you around because they feel their plans are better than yours. Nonetheless, you should be open to advice. You should be able to recognize good counsel and follow it. Find people who are more experienced and have succeeded in that endeavor. Seek their advice and compare it with your plan before drawing an inference. When you have people that can give you the tips you need to improve, it becomes easier to recover from a setback and forge ahead.

Common Obstacles to Building Resilience

No one wants to be mentally weak. We all want to be resilient and be able to weather the storm. However, this isn't often the case.

Below are some things that can keep you mentally weak regardless of your effort to build up strength mentally.

Getting Stuck to the Past

You cannot recover from a setback when you keep thinking about your past. Indeed, you are hurt, and it's natural to feel that way. You have devoted your time, energy, and money to the business or relationship, but it's now all futile. It's painful. However, you must move on. Moving on is the only good choice you can make out of the myriad of options you have.

Other options will only make you bound to something that is gone forever. Your adult child is gone. He or she might come back, but that shouldn't be your objective for now. You'll only continue to get angry and stir up negative emotions when you keep seeking reconciliation when the person doesn't want it. You cannot force yourself into people's lives. If anyone doesn't want you anymore, move on with your life. Imagine if JK Rowling kept crying every day because her husband divorced her, she would never have been able to produce Harry Potter. Don't have the notion that you cannot succeed without someone. Indeed, there are people who come into our lives that make the journey easier. Nonetheless, nobody is indispensable. Pessimism About the Future

When all you see about your future is darkness, doom, and bleakness, you cannot be resilient. You will always want to crawl into your shell to ruminate about the past because you don't have hope. What rule says that the remaining part of your life cannot be more glorious than all you have ever achieved in the past? It's not yet time to tell your story. Early bloomers often struggle when they have a major setback and because they are afraid that they would never get to the previous height again. Some of them feel that they were too quick to fulfil their potentials and have nothing left again. However, this is not true. If you keep seeking ways to improve yourself, you can always beat your previous records and set new ones.

Low Self-Efficacy

One of the things people who aren't resilient lack is the belief in their ability to succeed after a setback. Indeed, it can be a long road back to redemption, especially when you are facing tough times because of something bad you did. Nonetheless, you can rewrite history. Do it step by step but do it anyway. If you don't give up on yourself, the remaining part of your life can be the best part of it. Do you still remember the story of Colonel Sanders? If you are still living, you still have the chance to write the ending of the story of your life in a special way. No one might give you a chance for a comeback, but you need to back yourself. Everyone, including your friends and families, might write you off. However, it matters little if you refuse to give up on yourself. You'll eventually convince critics and doubters when you start getting the right results. Keep "singing," even when no one is dancing. Just be yourself, and people will eventually appreciate your uniqueness.

Lack of the Right Relationships

It's easier to bounce back from a setback when you have the right people around you. Indeed, determination is a crucial ingredient that can make a person stand his or her ground even when facing strong opposition. Nonetheless, you also need your loved ones. In other words, it's easier to believe you can pull through difficult times when you have people to offer you the needed support and encouragement. We cannot deny or underscore the support of friends and families in our journey in life. It can be devastating when you look around, and no one is willing to be in your corner during periods of need. You can feel lonely and rejected, which makes it difficult to be resilient. Our friends and families give us the courage and strength needed to overcome unpleasant situations. So, when they mock us or turn their backs on us when we are struggling, our strengths might fail us. Even when you don't have money, a cordial relationship with friends and family can see us through. However, when these people reject or keep reminding us about our past mistakes, it can become challenging to recover from a setback.

Lack of Focus

Keeping your focus during turbulent times is easier said than done. Nonetheless, you need it to find your way out of an emotional abyss. Take your time to find somewhere you can be free from distractions and carve out a new plan. One of the ways you can maintain your focus in life is by setting goals. Goals give you a sense of purpose and direction as you go about achieving them every day. Note that setting goals isn't all about writing out the things you want to achieve. Rather, there are some skills you need to learn that can make the process a success. Your goals must be specific and measurable. Besides, they should be relevant to you, achievable, and within a timeframe. Once your goals possess these attributes, you are on the right path.

Upward Social Comparison

Social comparison involves measuring your success by comparing yourself with people you feel are better than you or not up to your level. When you compare yourself with people that are below your level, it is a downward social comparison. However, it is an upward social comparison when you draw parallels with people you feel are better than you. Neither form of social comparison is healthy. However, the upward version is the worst. Upward social comparison hinders the development of resilience. You will keep looking at other people who have achieved the things you haven't achieved and feel bad about your life. This phenomenon is common in the modern world, thanks to social media. Many people post pictures of their expensive possessions to get remarks and comments. If you aren't careful, it can make you start feeling dissatisfied and frustrated about your life. So, when you are trying to recover from a setback, it is best for you to stay off social media to avoid developing negative emotions.

~ 32 ~

STRENGTH

You might have picked up this book because you felt your life was crashing. That perhaps you were a failure as a parent. Maybe you need to learn to grieve the loss of your child or children. Maybe you feel hopeless and lost. Maybe you're angry. Maybe you feel all these things in the same day, or even hour. Nonetheless, you can still build something glorious out of the ruins. YOU!!!

The tips below can help you recover from setbacks and forge ahead to make something beautiful out of the remaining part of your life.

Be Grateful

I have no idea what you have been through in your life. However, the truth is that it could have been worse. Yes! It left you heartbroken. You are mending your boat and still healing from the wounds, but it could have been worse than this. You need to start by seeing things from this perspective. Be grateful that you are still alive and still have a chance to do something with your life again. You might have lost a huge amount of money, but you still have your beautiful friends, a loving spouse, and others who genuinely care about you. So, be deliberately grateful. Get a journal and list out things in your life worth celebrating. Leave your home and go to places where you will find tranquility and just enjoy the ambiance. Go to the beach, mountain, or wherever you can connect with nature. Use those moments to value the basic things in life again – life, family, health. Breathe and stay in the moment as you prepare mentally to start all over again.

Surrender Is a Choice: Never Take It!

"If you fall behind, run faster. Never give up, never surrender, and revolt against the odds", Jesse Jackson. One of the statements you should never make in life is that you don't have a choice. It's not true because you always do. You can never be mentally strong when you leave yourself at the mercy of the circumstances surrounding you. As earlier mentioned, there are people in history or in the world today who have faced situations more limiting than yours and still succeeded in their endeavors. Therefore, surrendering is a choice people take, and you should never see it as an option. Those periods of your life when it seems your back is against the wall are the best opportunities to turn a corner by refusing to give up. Those times are the best periods to pick up biographies of people who have faced similar situations and learn from the way they were able to recover.

You Have Nothing to Lose Again

No one likes to fail, but failure is beautiful in some ways. In fact, it's good for your mental health sometimes. How? When you have never failed before, you are under considerable pressure to sustain your perfect record. You'll have many people thinking that you are superhuman, and that puts pressure on you. You want to maintain your status of invisibility, and that by itself can lead to anxiety. However, when something goes wrong, you and the people around you will realize that you are not impeccable, and that will reduce the level of pressure and expectations they have of you. At that point, you have nothing to lose again. Therefore, it is the perfect opportunity to do things without putting yourself under unnecessary pressure. You'll go about your business with a calm mind because you have nothing to prove to anyone. You are simply doing what you need to do to be the best version of yourself. So, when you fail, don't be too concerned about what people have to say about you. Whoever has not failed before should write you off. Obviously, there's no one like that.

Make New Friends

Friends are there for you on the days you are being celebrated. You share good times with them and enjoy the pleasant occasions. However, those are not the days you really need them. The days of adversity are the periods you need that arm around the neck and a bear hug the most. If your friends are not there for you as a rock, during your dark days, they don't deserve to be around you. You need to make new friends. Be around people who will give you the drive and positive energy you need to climb up the ladder again. Instead of sulking and wailing, talk to someone you know can encourage you. It helps a lot if the person has gone through that situation or something similar before. Remember to keep such people with you when the rainy days are over. It's unfortunate that some people have a culture of forgetting the people who were there for them during their moments of trial and tribulation. Don't be one of such ungrateful individuals. Share your pleasant moments with the friends who were there for you during your dark days.

Take a Step Back to Run Forward

There's no doubt that we all love it when people say nice things about us. This desire is the reason people post pictures of themselves on social media. We all want people to tell us how beautiful, elegant, and brilliant we are. However, it's a serious problem when those comments mean the world to you. It's one of the reasons some people struggle to recover after a setback. They cannot imagine not being in the spotlight again. You should learn to take a break sometimes to come up with a new strategy. This approach is particularly important after a major setback. Don't be under immense pressure to start doing something again. Take time and analyze the situation. Identify the areas where you made mistakes and think about how you could have done things differently. If you start again without learning your lessons, you'll make the same mistakes again.

Believe In Yourself Again

Your journey back to the top begins with forgiving yourself for making mistakes. You cannot undo what you have done. So, the best move is to let it go and try to make the best out of your life. Forgiving yourself will make you believe in yourself again. Note that you cannot succeed in any endeavor in life if you don't have self-confidence. It's natural that the thoughts of your past failures will run through your mind occasionally. Nonetheless, you should never let them limit you. To make things easier, ensure that you start by doing things you are confident you have mastery over. Leverage your strengths as you slowly build your self-esteem. It's not good for you to take another hit after a major crisis. So, it is safer to do things you are sure of before taking risks.

Resilience is a crucial ingredient that mustn't be missing in the life of anyone who wants to achieve his or her dream. Life will never give you what you want on a platter of gold. So, you must be determined and choose never to give up. You'll experience many challenges on your way to greatness. If you see them as stepping-stones to success, you will eventually become the best you can be. Otherwise, you will come back crashing to the ground. Life isn't about how many times you have failed. If you read the stories of great achievers, you'll notice that they weren't people who had it easy. Many of them have the odds stacked against them. Many of them were turned down by people who didn't believe in their dreams and ideas. However, they never allowed those moments to affect them. Instead, they defied the odds and faced their fears. They challenged the words of damning critics and were eventually able to prove them wrong. You can do the same too. You can choose to become stronger and build resilience from unfortunate situations you have found yourself in. Your story hasn't ended unless you choose to quit. Remember that the champions of today were once victims of adversity. However, they choose to learn from those periods to give themselves a better life. This is your opportunity to do the same. Take charge of your life and challenge the voices in your head telling you that you aren't cut out for the top.

If you are in any way feeling stuck or powerless in your life, there is a solution. You can choose to live in the NOW or The Present Moment. By understanding this skill and applying it to your life, you start slowing down the 'treadmill' of stress and pressure in your life. You're still running, you're still taking care of business, you're still being a responsible mature adult. That's not going to go away. The big difference is you become more aware, so you can become more content and fulfilled in the present moment. You're no longer kicking the can down the road when it comes to your personal happiness and fulfillment. You learn how to live in the present moment and enjoy it and accept it for what it is. Let me tell you, life is never going to be perfect. And if you are going to set yourself up where you will only agree to be happy when perfection enters your life, you're setting yourself up for a big letdown. This book teaches you the valuable skill of living in the moment. Not tomorrow, not next week, and not next year. Right here. Right now. I'm sure you already know this, but the moment you close this book, you might get hit by a truck. You might suffer some sort of weird and nasty medical allergic reaction. You might eat some bad food. There are all sorts of things that may cut your journey through this life short. Life is short. It is fragile, enjoy every moment. Hang on to it. Get a lot of meaning out of it. This is how you can keep running on that treadmill with a deep and abiding sense of peace and harmony within you.

~ 33 ~

FOCUS

Your focus is probably the most important factor in the process of overcoming whatever challenges you face. A lot of people think that they must have the right IQ, or they must be born with certain advantages, or some sort of other excuse. They think that there's all these circumstances and factors outside of them that would explain their success or lack of it. And unfortunately, the more you focus on things outside of you, and I'm talking about your circumstances as well as the situations you find yourself in or the people you surround yourself with, the more you lose sight of your focus. In fact, it can get so bad that you might ignore the power of your focus altogether. You might even completely forget how important personal focus is. Let's get one thing clear: what you choose to focus on, grows. If you don't believe me, look at people who hit the gym all day, every day. These are people who may be obese. These are people who may look like they're made from over-inflated dough. But the more they focus on working out, sticking to a certain diet and lifestyle, the sooner all that fat melts off. Similarly, people who focus on making money, sooner or later, end up achieving their dreams. People who focus on attracting members of the opposite sex tend to, later, connect the dots and meet with success more often than failure. In other words, you get out what you put in. What you focus on attracts your attention, which of course attracts your energy. When you devote energy to any kind of activity, sooner or later, you get good at it. Sure, in the beginning, it may look like it's impossible. It may look like it's just not going to happen. But the more you keep at it, the more you can figure things out. And, sooner or later, these baby steps turn into giant leaps forward. What you choose to focus on, grows. It doesn't matter what it is. It doesn't matter how seemingly impossible it may be. If you give it the proper focus, eventually, it will give way. I can't stress this enough. Unfortunately, people think that success is something that just falls into their lap. They think it's something that requires inhuman sacrifice and effort. No, it's not. Instead, it's just a choice of where you train your focus. The Good News Given how important focus is, I have some great news for you. Focus is a choice. That's right. It's not something that you're forced to do. It's not something that you are tricked into or somehow coerced by your circumstances. It's something that you can choose. If you can choose it, then this means you have control over it. There are so many other things you can choose to do, but you can choose to focus. This is power. This is control. This gives you some measure of input on how your life is going to turn out. Real Focus is Never Desperate A lot of people are under the impression that things will only change in their lives if they find themselves with their back against the wall. They think that once the chips are down and everything is desperate, that's when everything falls into place. What they're really doing is they're looking for excuse after excuse to avoid lifting a finger to change their circumstances. That's all you're doing if you believe that you must be pushed to decide. Real focus is never desperate. It is never the product of desperate times. It's something that you willfully choose and it's something that you choose consistently and continuously over an extended period. Don't think that it's some sort of magical superpower that you discover at the last minute. You will always have the power to choose, and you will always have the choice of focusing. It is never desperate, no matter how bleak the situation may look.

If you can wrap your mind around the idea that you can choose to focus, you can start reclaiming the power you get when you focus on certain things. Believe it or not, you can focus on your time to the extent that you can control the output you get when you spend your time on anything. I know this sounds crazy because most Americans think that there are not enough hours in a day. There are a lot of people who wish that there were more than 24 hours in a day. That's how pressed for time they are. What they're really suffering from, however, is a lack of focus. Believe it or not, you don't have to burn 8 hours at work to squeeze out 1 hour of productivity. Believe it or not, there are people out there who can put in 8 hours of work and get 8 hours of production. I know it sounds crazy, but that is the power of focus. Similarly, you don't have to waste a tremendous amount of your attention on many things in your life for you to maximize the results you get. You can focus intently on certain activities and have them produce a lot more results. You don't have to sit around worrying about certain things that may or may not happen. By deciding, giving it the proper attention, it deserves, and focusing the right number of resources and attention to detail, you end up getting the result you want without worrying yourself to death or mentally burning out. Finally, you can choose to focus your resources to such an extent that you get a lot more bang out of every buck you spend. One of the main reasons why Americans are trillions of dollars in credit card debt is because of inefficient spending. The problem isn't spending. The big challenge is that they spend on many things trying to get some sort of outcome. They didn't know that if they spent on the right things, they would have spent less money and gotten into less debt while getting a lot more results. You must reclaim your ability to focus on all these to start living a life of power, purpose, meaning and direction. Unfortunately, people who end up struggling by moving a lot while staying in the same place suffer from a total lack of focus or fuzzy focus. The Bottom Line The bottom line with focus is straightforward. You only have so much mental resources in any given second. Make it count. Learn the skills that you need to get the most out of the time that you put into any kind of activity, the attention that you put into any kind of project, or the resources you devote to your plans. If you're able to do this, you start to reclaim your life. Rediscover the Eternal Now I know what you're thinking. You're probably rolling your eyes and saying to yourself, "Yeah, it's very easy. Just focus." I understand your skepticism. There is kind of a hollow ring to the phrase "Just focus." It's not all that far from " Just do it," the famous Nike slogan. But when you dig deeper, it's all you need to know regarding how to achieve greater control over your life. Focus means directing your attention. Because where your attention goes, your time, resources and personal energy flows. And it all boils down to something that you have a tremendous amount of control over your attention. Therefore, it's important to rediscover the concept of "The Eternal Now." Believe it or not, you are always living in the present moment. When a second passes, the next second is the present moment. Once that's up, the next second is the present moment. Now, a lot of people think this is pointless. After all, that's how time is supposed to work. But they miss the big picture. They miss the fact that when you are in the moment, there are a lot of things that are possible within that frame of time. We're not just talking about time and space. We're talking about mental, spiritual and physical states. If you don't believe in the present moment and you think it's just a means to an end, it's easy to blow through your time. Seriously. It's easy to live through time in a way that you're not really paying attention to the things you should be focusing on. Sadly, most people have forgotten the present moment. They're all in a rush to be somewhere. They're all in a rush to become somebody else. They start looking at themselves primarily as transitory beings. In other words, who you are right here, right now, is something that you're not really all that happy with. Instead, you want to be somebody who is 50 pounds lighter, 10 years younger, $10 million richer, and so on and so forth. Your focus is burned up by the overarching need to go somewhere and become somebody else. The concept of the present moment completely escapes you except for certain schedules or dates or appointments. But other than that, it's just some sort of temporal steppingstone to who "you are supposed to be." Therefore, so many people seem so busy, preoccupied and obsessed with motion. They can't wait to get from Point A to Point B. The problem is desiring motion and that alternative identity of who we could be exacts a heavy price. They leave us empty. The Eternal Now, which is one of the greatest gifts anybody can give us, is worthless to us. We look at it as basically a byproduct of living and not really a goal in and of itself. This is too bad. How come? The Eternal Now is the foundation of your future. It is the birthplace of who you can be and what you can become. In other words, it is the foundation of possibility and being.

Meditation Reveals the Power of the Eternal Now

When you practice meditation and mindfulness, you tap into the power of The Eternal Now. First, you become aware that you are living in a present moment. Once you can do that, you then slowly but surely come face to face with the power of your mind to shape your reality. Instead of constantly trying to zip from one mental place to another, you realize that there's power where you are. You realize that you have all that it takes to get out from under whatever it is that's frustrating you. It doesn't matter how stuck you may feel, if you are able to tap into the power of The Eternal Now, you can use the present moment to achieve important changes in your life. Best of all, you're able to this right here, right now. You break away from the old and familiar game of kicking the can of your happiness down the road. You can choose to be happy, fulfilled and content right here, right now. All it takes is to train the way your mind is already configured to rediscover and celebrate The Eternal Now.

It's easy to look at mindfulness and meditation as simply tools that you use on your journey of grieving and recovery. Fair enough.

But it's very important to understand what it is you want in the first place. Let's put it this way, even if you were equipped with the most powerful equipment in the world, if you don't know where you're going, your trip would be pointless. Chances are, you would be chasing your tail and be going around in circles. The world existed before you, it exists now while you're in it, and will continue to exist long after you're gone. So do your adult children. You must be at peace with this eternal truth. To fully wrap your minds around this, I need you to understand certain truths about how human beings have historically looked at the world and their place in it. With this understanding, your mind should be big enough to see your real place.

Everything Works in Duality

Did you know that everything in the world, both seen and unseen, works in duality? You can't have black without white. You can't have empty without full. You can't have up without down. You can't have in without out. This is not an empty and shallow mental exercise. Instead, these dualities speak to the fundamental truth of what gives life meaning and power. The Greeks got it partially right. Their philosophy is binary in nature. Male and female, good and evil, light and dark, and so on and so forth. The problem is, the Greeks focused primarily on the 'good things,' the ideals, the forms, the essence. When they did this, they basically sidelined the other half of the equation. It is a binary world. They got that part right. But by focusing only on the positives on the matter at the expense of the antimatter, of light at the expense of the darkness, they stripped away a significant portion of the power of duality. In fact, the Western mind has historically viewed the other side of these equations as suspect or weak or somehow untrustworthy. It's easy to celebrate the masculine side of a personality, but we're suspicious about the feminine side. It's easy to see the value of the light, but we're scared of the darkness. Do you see how this works? This is the Greek or Western mindset. Yin and Yang

Make the Universe Turn

Thankfully, there is an alternative to the Greek black and white mindset. I am, of course, talking about the Chinese idea of yin and yang. When you look at the yin and yang symbol, it's obvious that it acknowledges the binary nature of reality. But unlike Westerners, the Chinese see an equal value in the other side of the equation. They understand that "full", or "substance" would be meaningless without the complementary reality of "emptiness" or "nothingness." One good example of this is in the Tao Te Ching, the primary scripture of Taoism, where it highlights the importance of the empty hole in a pot. Usually, people don't even think about the empty hole in the pot. They think about how big the pot is, they think about the price, they think about what the pot is made of. Usually, people don't think about the empty hole. But the Tao Te Ching points out that it's the emptiness inside that pot that gives that pot value. After all, that's where you store stuff. A solid pot with no hole in the middle is completely worthless. In other words, it's the void or the nothingness that exists in a binary relationship with "somethingness" that gives life value. The Chinese get it. They understand that the darkness is not to be feared. They understand that emptiness is not something to cry over. It all depends on context and how the seemingly negative elements work with other factors. This is how you get a big picture of the eternal. You go past duality and understand and ultimately embrace the power of the void. A lot of Americans fear death. They're scared of the good times ending. A lot of people don't like to watch movies end, but believe it or not, death is what gives life meaning. Let's put it this way, if you knew you were going to live forever, do you think you would live a life of meaning? Do you think you would be kind to people? Do you think you would look to heal the wounds of your past? Do you think you would try to be compassionate and understanding? Of course, not. When you get a deadline, you get perspective. The idea of duality communicates this loud and clear. You can't just live your life looking at the "something" of life. These are things that you can see, touch, taste, smell and hear. You should also pay attention to the void. This is something that you can only grasp with your mind, but it's real, nonetheless. It complements the something to produce real power in your life. The key that turns the ignition on this process, however, is focus.

Your Mental Self-Reclamation Blueprint

This power of mindfulness and mental focus will help people reclaim their lives. It doesn't matter whether you are feeling stuck, feeling frustrated, or you just feel that your life is meaningless. When you follow this blueprint, you start living your life with a renewed sense of purpose. Why? You gain perspective. It turns out that if you're like most people, you spend your life in such a way where you're pouring a tremendous amount of your focus and energy on things that keep you stuck. You don't devote them to things and activities that can take you where you want to go. You must reclaim yourself because nobody else is going to do it for you. It doesn't matter how much they say they love you; it doesn't matter how much they say they know you or accept you, at the end of the day, everybody's got enough problems of their own. You must do this yourself. You must take the initiative. Nobody else will do it for you.

One Final Word

This book is not magic, not mysticism, nor does it involve religion, except in a higher power of your understanding, or your disbelief in such. The techniques work with how your mind is already configured. You're not doing something new to your brain. You're just tapping abilities that you already have. It really all boils down to shifting your focus and your energy. Everything else will flow because your mind already has these abilities. Zero in on your life's objective to truly reclaim your life by focusing on living in the moment, you must have a destination.

Remember, the ability to live in the present moment is just a tool. It's just a practice that you use to achieve some sort of objective. Don't confuse the two. A lot of people think that if you practice mindfulness, meditation or engage in any sort of activity that helps you fully utilize the moment, then you are living life to the fullest. That's not true. You still must have objectives, goals and a destination. With that said, knowing the power of living in the moment makes the process so much more meaningful. Instead of just simply chasing your tail and ending up this mental fog, every moment feels like an adventure. It feels that you're doing something with your life. It feels that you were put on this earth for a reason. That's a very empowering feeling. It is the 180-degree opposite of feeling stuck, feeling like another face in the crowd or feeling like your life really has no meaning. The moment that you start thinking that your life has no meaning or purpose, it becomes very easy to imagine life without you. In other words, it's easy to think that you are an accident or whether you live, or die doesn't really matter because you're not making that much of an impact. You see the rabbit hole that you fall into once you start that line of thinking. The mental self-reclamation plan that you're following starts with the most important part. It answers the question why. The problem with life is that a lot of people are focused on answering what, when and how. Don't get me wrong. These are important questions to ask, but they must lead somewhere. They're preliminary questions. They're not the final question. The final question is why. This is all about understanding your understanding of the meaning of life. I know that's kind of a funky sentence, but that's the best we can do. At the end of the day, life is our understanding of what life is about. It's not like you can investigate the purest form of reality of life. Again, this is not mysticism. This is not a religion. Instead, this is practical psychology. What we're looking at is your perception or your read of the ultimate objective of your life. Now, this might seem like a tall order at this point, and I would agree with you. It's like trying to unravel a thick ball of yarn in one step. It usually doesn't work that way. You must slowly unwind that ball and this where the following process comes in. Take a mental inventory at any given second, what are you thinking about? What are you worried about? What do you obsess over? What do you focus on? Write all this down and record the first thing that comes to your mind. There are no right or wrong answers. What's important is you just write down everything that comes to your mind. Get it in writing. Do you see a pattern? Do you focus primarily on process instead of objectives or vice versa? Do you focus on timelines instead of the things you're supposed to do? Again, there's no right or wrong answer. I just want you to be aware of the things and concerns that you carry around in your mind every single moment. For this reason, I quit all my Estranged Parent Support Groups. I was guilty of spending too much energy on the loss of my adult children That was my focus and that needed to be changed.

When you do a mental inventory, it's as if you brush your pet. Throughout the day, your pet will pick up certain debris from your yard, from your carpet, from any interior space of your home. But when you brush the fur of your pet it ends up with a fresh coat. It ends up clean. The same applies to your mind. If you don't do a mental inventory, you'd be surprised as to how cluttered, clogged and overburdened your mind gets. It's as if you're living your life day to day and you're picking up all these worries, concerns and anxieties and you are the last person to know.

Take a Focus inventory

Your mental inventory is kind of a broad survey of what you stuff into your mind. The next step is to drill a little deeper. We're going to be a little bit more particular. In this step, we're going to look at what you devote your focus on. In any given second, where does your focus mostly go? Are you focused on things that happened in the past or are you worrying about things that have yet to happen? Are you focused on the tasks immediately ahead of you? Do you spend a lot of time thinking about whether you've forgotten something or not? Do you feel anxious about forgetting something or not doing something that you're supposed to be doing? Or are you focusing on your loss as I was? Again, there's no right or wrong answer here. There's no one-size-fits-all solution. Just write down what you spend your focus on. It's important to note that different people focus on different things. People, after all, have different priorities. We have different values. We come from different backgrounds. We also have different experiences.

Take a life inventory

For some people, this is going to get a little bit uncomfortable. For this stage, I want you to write down what you think you've achieved with your life. It doesn't matter whether you're 20 years old, 40 years old or 80 years old. It doesn't matter whether you have a degree, you dropped out of high school, you have a couple of million dollars to your name. Just write down what you think what you have achieved in your life. It doesn't have to presently exist. Maybe it's an experience that you had. Maybe one of your greatest personal achievements was you visited Rome, Italy or Paris, France. Write that down. Whatever you think you have achieved, list it. Again, this should be a stream of consciousness exercise, so don't edit yourself, don't think that an answer is stupid or doesn't have a place on your list. Just write down whatever comes to mind. If it feels like it answers the question, list it down.

What truly matters?

Now, at this point, you're going to do some sorting. You understand that your life has an objective. With your objective firmly in mind, look at your mental inventory list, your focus inventory sheet and your life inventory tally. Go through all those listings with your life's objective in mind. Always refer to your ultimate objective as you read through these materials. Get comfortable with the objective as your primary frame of reference. Use that razor Now, here comes the tough part. Look at all your different lists and then start scratching out items that do not lead to your grand objective. You plan is simple. Either it leads you to the objective or you lose it. In other words, on all the lists that you have set up, cut out things that are obviously not going to lead you to your objective. That is your goal. Because if you were to do this, you practice personal clarity where everything in your life leads to one place and one place alone. I remember the first time I did this; it was quite eye-opening. If anything, it made me realize that a lot of the things I was working for, a lot of things that I spent a tremendous amount of emotional, financial and physical resources on were pointless. It's like being assigned a big project at work and you spend most of your time checking your Facebook updates, your Instagram feed and your emails. Don't get me wrong. At some level or other, those tasks are important. But ultimately, you're not going to keep your job depending on how well you answer your email. You're not going to get a raise because you are very prompt in checking up on your Facebook notifications. Am I making sense? Focus on what's important. Focus on what you are here for. In other words, zero in on your life's objective and make sure your mental inventory, your focus inventory and your life inventory line up to grand objective. If you were to do this, you'd start living a life of meaning, direction and purpose.

Previously, I talked about identifying your life's objective. This is a very exhilarating process because as I've mentioned, it's too easy to live your life like a lost person. You think you have a purpose; you think you are trying hard, you are being a mature and responsible adult, but it's it turns out that despite how hard you try and how much you plan and how seemingly focused you think you are, you end up going around in circles. This, of course, is because you don't really have a grand objective. Previously, you zeroed in on the grand objective of your life. You zeroed in what you want your life to produce. Think of it this way, when people show up to your funeral and they see your body in a box, what would you want people to think about the life you lived? Would you like them to say he/she was a kind person, or he/she helped a lot of people, or he/she revolutionized the world or discovered something? Think about those things. This should form your grand objective because you're using other people's impressions of you as some sort of objective mirror for what you think you want for yourself. Now, if that seems clear enough, here's a monkey wrench. You must ask yourself, "Are my grand objectives really mine?" I know this seems kind of a bit of a letdown because, we talked about the great revelation of your life's meaning or central focus. However, we can't do this blindly. We can't just say, "Because I do have this grand objective, then that's all I need to focus on." Well, there's another level of analysis. You must ask yourself, "Is this really mine or did I just pick it up from somebody else?" This is not an easy process to go through. It requires some preliminary steps.

Do a memory detox

A lot of people think they have grand objectives because they have certain memories of the past that lead to these objectives. Maybe you remember telling your mom that when you grow up, you'll be an attorney, a doctor or a politician. Maybe you told your dad that when you become a grown up, you'll be a professional athlete. These are heartwarming when people say them now, but are they based on the truth? Do a memory detox. In other words, when you say your grand objective to yourself, think of memories that these triggers. Zero in on one memory and ask yourself, "Did this really happen?" Often many of our memories aren't accurate. It is believed that every time we access a memory, we change that memory. Now, if the answer is yes, you're going to analyze it some more. But if the answer is no, then you need to start having second thoughts about your grand objective. This might be an assumed memory. You don't want to build a house on a foundation of sand. Now, assuming that memory is based on facts and things did happen, ask yourself, "Am I exaggerating things?" You must remember that people say stuff all the time, but what we choose to remember might be quite different from what took place. Ask yourself, "Do I remember this correctly or is this exaggerated? Am I blowing things out of proportion?" Again, if this is the case, then you need to be suspicious of your grand objective. It might be based on fiction or exaggeration. Neither of these is good. If it isn't exaggerated, ask yourself if there are missing pieces of the memory. If this is the case, then be very suspicious. You might be filling in the memories to produce a certain mental state that you are looking for. This usually happens in cases of abuse. Whether mental or physical, they kind of work the same. It was so traumatic that you only remember in fragments. You must detoxify your memory. Finally, if your memory is based on fact, ask yourself, "Is this the only interpretation? Are there any other grand objectives I can derive from this memory? Please don't get me wrong. I'm not saying that you are not entitled to your personal grand objective. I'm not trying to rob you of your big dreams. However, all I'm doing is walking you through the process of realizing what your grand objectives rest on. Are they real memories or are you exaggerating them? Are you filling stuff in or are you just interpreting them to lead to a certain outcome? Just be aware of how this plays out, so you end up totally owning your life's grand objectives. You start seeing it with your plain eyes. You don't choose to filter it with rose-colored glasses.

Do an attitude detox

Memory is one thing, attitude is another. Believe it or not, your attitude plays a big role in how your life turns out. If your attitude is that of a victim, then you find yourself feeling small, stuck, powerless. Worse yet, you feel that you are life's martyr. Everybody takes turns victimizing you. You feel disrespected and deep down you don't really feel worthy of respect. The worst part of all of this is if you feel like some sort of victim, it's too easy to excuse yourself to be harsh or even cruel to other people. After all, if you're hurting so badly, it's too easy to get numb to the pain so that you lose sight the pain you, yourself, dish out. Try to explain your attitude to yourself. Given what's happening in your life, are there any other ways to interpret what's going on? For example, if you think your job is a daily humiliation where you clock in, spend 8 hours, and then clock out, ask yourself, "Is this the only way to look at this situation?" My job does give me a paycheck. I do hang around with interesting people. I do get to use my muscles or my brain for my work. Obviously, it's interesting enough, otherwise I would have quit a long time ago. Ask yourself, "Is the way I'm looking at this part of my life the most optimal one?" This is really an indirect way of asking yourself, "What is my attitude?" The problem with attitude is, sometimes, they're like sunglasses that we put on and we forgot that we have them on. Everywhere you turn seems like everything is a little dark. But it turns out, things look that way because you have your 'mindset' sunglasses on. Your attitude works the same way. You might think that you're just perceiving your reality or living your life, and everything is objectively neutral. No, they're not. Everything you perceive from the outside world is filtered through the prism or lens or your attitude. Believe it or not, if you change your attitude, the world's appearance and your perception of your world starts to change. You can either look at the end of the tunnel as the beginning of freedom or you could look at that light at the end of the tunnel as a train headed your way. These are two totally different things courtesy of differences in attitude. I need you to do an attitude detox. I want you to take off your lens or filter and look at what's going on in your life in the most objective way possible. Is it really that bad? Are your relationships really that poisonous? Is your childhood really that messed up? Oftentimes, the limitation that we feel hold us back and drag us down are chosen. They're not chosen by other people, mind you, you chose them. You wear those invisible shackles by choice. Reclaim your power to choose You must understand that your life is a choice. I hate to break it to you. The way you dress, even your IQ, how much money you have in the bank, how good you look, the style of your hair, the size of your car, the size of your house, whether you rent or own a house and all the other details of your life, all those are choices. A lot of people would have a problem with this. After all, who in their right mind would choose to be poor, oppressed or burdened? Who in their right mind would choose to live a life of powerlessness and limited choices? Well, these are illusions. Ultimately, your external life, I'm talking about things that people can readily observe, is a product of your internal choices. If you start choosing internal realities differently, sooner or later, they will bubble up to the surface. It's not going to happen overnight, but these changes are undeniable if they're consistent. If your mind has totally shifted direction, sooner or later, your thoughts will be manifest in the reality you live. You start dressing differently. You start talking about different things. You start expressing a different kind of attitude. Sooner or later, you start behaving differently.

The world doesn't care about your feelings. It really doesn't care at all about your emotions. The world doesn't care that you have certain emotional issues and that's why you're 50 pounds overweight. All the world sees is that you have extra weight. The world doesn't know nor care that you fear certain things and that's why you have the job that you have and pays very little. All it sees is a person making very little money. That's why it's important to reclaim your power to choose because, ultimately, if you want your life to change and produce certain outcomes, these will all flow from your internal choices. Therefore, it's important to make those internal choices. There are only really three questions that you need to wrap your mind around. What are your ideals? What are your values? Does everything line up? Only you can answer these questions. Everybody is different. Some people are content with a few bucks and food on the table. Other people want to travel. They want to learn all they can learn. They want to experience the very best that life has to offer. Others like challenges. They like adventure. They like to discover new worlds. Again, everybody is different, but what's important is that you are mindful of what you want for yourself. What's important is that you have a clear idea of what your purpose is.

Unfortunately, when you think that you have a grand objective, chances are you picked this up somewhere. It's not unusual for children to live the lives of their parents. It's not unusual for children to inherit the conflicts and frustrated ambitions of their parents. I'm telling you; life is too short for that. You shouldn't live your life for your parents or your children. You should live your life for yourself. They all had their chance. Let that go. Focus on what makes sense to you. This is your purpose. You have all these dead-lines and big projects that need to be completed. Unfortunately, the more you complete them, the thicker the fog. Eventually, it starts to dawn on you that what you're doing is pointless. It doesn't matter how "mission critical" the project is. It doesn't matter how much money you will make with the project. You still end up in the same place. When you live with purpose, all this fog clears up and you see that straight line to where you'd like to go. Similarly, purpose flows from integrity.

Integrity is one word you don't hear much nowadays. Usually, when people use the word integrity, they often talk about the ability to tell the truth. They talk about living life with character. While that's important and everything, I use the word integrity in a very limited sense. When you live with integrity, you focus like a laser on the outcomes you would like for your life, and you act accordingly. Everything you do leads to that outcome. That is a life of integrity because your actions line up with your ideals, your values and your grand objectives. Believe it or not, living life with integrity and prizing integrity, leads to a real life. You feel like your actions have consequences. You feel that every moment that you waste chasing your tail has a consequence and just like having some sort of personal GPS, you keep getting redirected to where you need to go. Each step that you take has more meaning. It's not just something that you do as part of the course. You don't feel like you're just going through the motions. In fact, if you become so disciplined, every breath you take feels like an opportunity and a blessing at the same time. That's the power of a life of integrity, flowing from purpose.

Get Quiet

What if I told you that you're always interrupting yourself? What if I told you that you have a conscious goal and a subcon-scious mind? What if you get your wires crossed? What if you think you are pursuing certain goals and then up sabotaging yourself or undermining yourself? This happens quite a bit. People think that they are being focused, that they have a set goal in mind that they are doing things intentionally. Unfortunately, for the life of them, nothing seems to work. They think that they're going through the right process and they're focusing on the right things, but regardless of how much time, effort and energy they put in, they keep tripping up, things take a lot longer, they make serious mistakes, it takes a lot more effort. In many cases, they end up in a far worse spot than when they started. What's going on? Well, it boils down to people interrupting themselves. They can't help it. They feel that they just go through their thought process in an automatic or semiautomatic way only to produce the same results each time. To break free of this, you only need to do one thing: get quiet. I know it sounds simplistic. A lot of people will quickly dismiss this idea, but the truth is if you get quiet first a lot of the things that you're struggling with become easier. You start getting a big picture view of what it is you're doing despite your conscious goals and objectives. You put yourself in a position where it becomes easier for you to take action that will finally get you out of the tough spot, you're in. It all boils down to deciding to get quiet first.

Stop Editing Your Thoughts

One common way people trip themselves up and interrupt their ability to focus so clearly that they turn their thoughts into reality involves editing. Believe it or not you're constantly editing your thoughts. Maybe this is due to other people's expectations of you. Perhaps you're thinking of thoughts that you think you shouldn't be thinking. Possibly, you are willfully trying to impose a certain interpretation on your thoughts. Whatever the case may be you're engaged in one form of editing or other. Stop it. Your first goal should be to think as clearly as possible. You don't really know what your real thoughts are when you're always editing them. How can you get a clear understanding of your mental processes when you can't even bring yourself to admit the raw, uncut, unfiltered version of your thoughts? You quickly realize that there's really nothing to apologize for. Sure, you may be thinking about horrible stuff. This stuff might even be embarrassing or trigger some sort of guilt from the past, but they're your thoughts. Nobody can see them. They only exist in your mind. Let them flow. Stop trying to filter them. Stop trying to warp, distort or somehow control them. Instead, focus on clarity. What exactly are you thinking? It may be scary at first but that's a small price to pay for the power that will arise from clarity. Choose to be clear first. Stop editing your thoughts.

Stop Editing Your Feelings

When thoughts flash in your mind, it's too easy to try to impose some sort of meaning onto it. In other words, it's too tempting to analyze them as they materialize. The reason people do this is because thoughts are never emotionally neutral. Once a thought appears in your mind, it triggers a range of emotions. This can be positive or negative, but there are always feelings involved. It is no surprise that once people perceive some sort of mental image, they quickly jump to the feelings that they're getting and guess what? They try to control those feeling. It's like when you're walking through a mall holding hands with your kid and you see another person. Maybe this person looks unusual or is wearing something odd. Your kid starts to laugh, and you turn around and tell your kid not to laugh. That's what you're doing with your feelings. You perceive certain things in your mind, and you know that you have developed an emotional reaction, so you try to stop or edit that feeling. Either you're trying to cut it out altogether or reshape it to something more acceptable or something more expected. This is a problem because when you do that, you're not being honest. If a certain mental image flashes in your mind or a certain memory appears in your head, let the emotions come. There's nothing to be embarrassed about. There's nothing to apologize for. These are your emotions. Again, your first objective is to be as clear as possible regarding what you're feeling. Later, you can work on implications. You can work on focusing on what this all leads to as well as lining these up with your grand life objectives.

Watch Your Thoughts like Clouds

One of the best ways to get quiet on different levels is to simply watch your thoughts like clouds. Here's how you do it. Find a dark room, make sure that you won't be interrupted for at least fifteen minutes, close your eyes and slowly breathe in and out deeply. After about three to five repetitions, you should be feeling relaxed. Next, focus your mind's eye on the thoughts appearing in your mind. Once the images appear, do not interpret them. Do not analyze them. Just watch them. This means you're going to acknowledge them, but you're not going to judge them. These are two totally different things. For example, when you were a kid in elementary school, maybe you got abused by bullies. Perhaps there was a guy named Jeff who was harsh on you, and, for the longest time, you always remember Jeff and you feel really, negative, angry, upset, powerless when the mental image of Jeff appears in your mind. When you watch your thoughts like clouds, you let Jeff's image appear. Just like a cloud overhead. But instead of allowing yourself to instantly feel angry, upset or feel powerless and weak, you let Jeff's image come. You acknowledge to yourself that is Jeff from junior high. Notice how neutral that statement is? You didn't follow it up with "That was my oppressor in junior high. That is the guy who stole my childhood. That is the guy who makes me feel so weak and stupid to this very day." You don't say any of that. Instead, you just say that's Jeff. When you do that, you take ownership of the memory. This happened. This is part of you whether you like it or not. Most importantly, you don't impose any judgment on him. Just like a cloud passing by, it's neither good nor bad. It's just passing by. Let it pass through. When you do this, you take power over your mental state. You then count your breath, and you repeat the process with another memory. This way, with enough repetition, your memories no longer have a negative hold on you. You no longer feel triggered so that you respond in a very negative emotional way. You feel in control. It's not like you're denying these memories or sweeping them under the rug. You accept them. They happen but you let them pass. Sooner or later, it dawns on you that these negative memories that you did not choose, by the way, don't have to have a hold on you. They don't have to bring out the very worst in you. Instead, just like clouds, they appear and then they disappear and pass on. Sooner or later, if you keep repeating this and you plug into the quite calm made possible by your breathing exercise, you start having a more productive relationship with your past as well as your future. How come? Well, you can also effectively deal with your worries about the future using the technique above. It all boils down to saving the eternal moment. When you focus on the present moment right here, right now, you get power because in this very second, you don't have to do things the same way you've always done them. You don't have to feel sad when the mental image of your father who broke a broom on your back when you were a kid flashes into mind. You just say, "That's my dad". You don't have to step into a rabbit hole of rage when the picture of your mom who slapped you in front of a lot of people when you were all of five years old flashes in your mind. You just say, "That's my mom". Do you see how this works? That's the power of the eternal moment because the eternal moment gives you choice. Finally, if you keep repeating this process, you stop chasing after answers. You stop asking "Why? Why me? Of all the kids, why did I have to live that life?" and other related questions. Once you stop chasing after the answers and you practice getting quiet, you quickly realize that the answers come to you instead.

Refocus

Practice mindfulness to reclaim your power of focus. The reason you're feeling stuck, powerless, weak and confused is because your focus is going to where it shouldn't go. Remember where your focus goes, energy flows. Whatever you focus on grows. So, if you focus on things that upset you, make you feel small, make you feel weak or otherwise make you feel flawed, you end up amplifying your negative emotions and judgments. Be careful where you invest focus. Therefore, it's important to practice mindfulness. Here are some techniques.

Counting Your Breath

The most basic way to practice mindfulness is to simply count your breath. You just need to close your eyes, find yourself in a quiet room and just count your breath. Count the breath coming in and coming out. Eventually, you should focus your attention on the part of your nostrils that the air is coming out of. That's all you should notice. You stop focusing on the appearance of things around you. You stop paying attention to the sounds around you. You just focus on the air slowly coming in and out of your nose. This heightens your focus and awareness. A lot of people think that when they slow their minds down to a standstill that they're eventually going to fall asleep. Well, if you feel sleepy, you're doing it wrong. Believe it or not when you're counting your breath or practicing any kind of mindfulness exercise, you're super-aware. It's kind of like drinking five cups of coffee for your brain but without the frantic nervousness.

Breathe-Hold-Breathe

This mindfulness technique was originally formulated for US Navy SEALs looking to relax during highly sensitive combat missions. If you are a SEAL Team member, a lot of lives are depending on how well you do your job. It goes without saying that these guys have a lot of pressure on them. Talk about a stressful job. The breathe-hold-breathe technique enables Navy SEALs soldiers to quickly relax right before they make a very important action. Maybe they're going into a firefight. Perhaps they're about to go into the water and dive for an extended period or possibly they're going to be doing something very sensitive involving explosive. Whatever the case may be they need to relax so they can focus right here, right now. Most importantly, they need to relax ASAP. Breathe-hold-breathe delivers instant peace of mind guaranteed. How does it work? Breathe slowly and deeply out, hold for four to eight seconds and then slowly breathe back in and then hold for four to eight seconds and repeat this process several times. With enough slow repetition, you feel really, really relaxed and, most importantly, you feel focused. All distractions leave you. The best part to all of this is that you can do this very quickly. It doesn't take much time. Usually, for most people, it takes anywhere from three to six repetitions to get relaxed enough so they can do what they need to do.

Secular Transcendental Meditation

Transcendental meditation is somewhat controversial in some circles. A lot of people have second thoughts about this mindfulness practice. It really is too bad because transcendental meditation is one of the most powerful meditation techniques you can ever adopt if you are looking to let go of painful memories or useless present worries or otherwise are seeking a deep reservoir of inner peace. The confusion arises from transcendental meditation's use of mantras. Mantras, after all, have historically been used by Buddhists and Hindus as part of their meditation practice. This raises a red flag to a lot of people who are looking for a mindfulness technique that is completely secular and non-religious. Well, a lot of people overlook the fact that transcendental meditation is all about using nonsense words as mantras. This is the key. In fact, if you study transcendental meditation, its teachers actively discourage people from using words that have meaning as their mantra. The whole point of transcendental meditation is for your mind to destroy thoughts. You're so focused on the present moment that you cannot even form thoughts. That's how powerful and relaxing transcendental meditation can be. It is secular, but people miss the memo on that so once they hear the word "mantra", all sorts of mystical imagery come to their minds. It really is too bad because like I said transcendental meditation is one of the most powerful mindfulness practices out there. Here's how it works. Find a quiet room that you will not be disturbed in. Reserve that room for at least fifteen minutes. Find a comfortable place to sit and just sit. No need to assume the lotus position. No need to take a pose like some sort of Buddhist or Hindu mystic. There's no need to do that. You're not practicing yoga. You're just relaxing. Sit normally. Once you've done that, close your eyes and follow the instructions for counting your breath. You must enter that deep level of relaxation. Once you get to that point, the next time you breathe in, say a word that doesn't have any meaning to you. You can say "shoosh" or something like that. It must be a word that has absolutely no meaning. After you've done that, hold your breath for half a second so you can focus on the word that you just said and then breathe out and say the word again. Eventually, you will hit a pattern where you are paying attention to your repetition of the mantra. If you keep this up long enough, you reach a point where you're not developing thoughts. The moment a thought starts to form, it gets destroyed by your mantra. If you keep this up long enough over an extended period in many practice sessions, you feel a deep, deep sense of peace and inner harmony. There's nothing to be afraid of. There's no future to worry about. All you have is the present moment.

Embrace the Moment

Regardless of the meditation technique or mindfulness practice you adopt, make sure they all lead to the same place. Make sure they all enable you to embrace the moment. Rediscover the eternal now. The key here is to occupy the space around you with your presence. I'm not talking about your physical presence. I'm talking about your mental presence. This is how your awareness can help you achieve greater levels of peace, serenity and calm. When you're in this space, you appreciate it for its emptiness. You don't have to be anybody. You don't have to go anywhere. That's right. No one to be nowhere to go. When you're able to wrap your mind around these concepts, you don't feel left behind. You don't feel like you're missing out on something. Instead, you feel complete.

Operate Out of Freedom

If you practice the techniques above correctly, you will learn to operate out of your mental free space. This is a tremendous process for letting go unnecessary stress and drama of your life. You no longer look at your thoughts as something you deal with, or you no longer look at your goals as "something to do". Instead, you stop compartmentalizing your life and you realize that every single moment is a gift. It's an opportunity. It ties you in to the eternal now, which is full of potential.

Scale

In the beginning, making progress achieving inner peace may seem like an uphill climb. This is perfectly natural. After all, you're working against your habits. This is not how your mind is normally set up. As I mentioned earlier, everything in your life is a choice. As unhealthy as your current thinking patterns may be, at the end of the day, you chose them at some earlier point in time. Now that you've read this book, you are deprogramming yourself. Hopefully. Don't expect a lot on Day 1 or even Day 100. Just take it one day at a time. Eventually, as you get used to it, things will start to improve. Things get easier and easier over time. Eventually, you will be able to achieve a deep sense of inner peace. At first, this inner peace is something that you experience when you are consciously practicing mindfulness. This means you schedule a certain amount of time at a specific place when you do it. However, once it becomes second nature to you and you know the steps like the back of your hand, you can then let your inner peace spread to other areas of your life. Please understaffed that the skills that you learn in managing your thoughts can apply the across the board. You can apply it to your relationships, your body image, your personal ambitions and goals and everything else. Living with Integrity Once you have achieved a tremendous amount of peace and focus thanks to the art of learning how to be quiet, you can then start to live with integrity. You know what your grand objectives are. Everything must line up to it; otherwise, you're not living a life of integrity. The good news is when everything lines up, every day is an adventure. Every day is full of great promise. Every day can lead to happiness and joy. Please note that this happiness and joy are not something that you enjoy in the distant future or after you achieve certain things. No. You enjoy them in the here and now. From inner peace comes real confidence because everything lines up. Everything has meaning. Everything has purpose. Create an Upward Spiral When you work from confidence, you become more competent. This is obvious. Why? Well, when you're confident, you try a lot more things. When you try a lot more things, sometimes you fail; sometimes you succeed but, sooner or later, you learn how to succeed more often than you fail. This then leads to greater competence because now you can do things the right way, so you succeed more often, which then makes you feel more confident. You're able to try out more and experiment more, which leads to even greater levels of confidence, competence and on and on it goes. Living a life of confidence and competence thanks to the power of integrity takes time, focus and energy. This book lays out a solid plan that anybody can follow to reclaim their lives after family estrangement. It doesn't matter what your past looks like. It doesn't matter how small, weak, powerless and voiceless you feel now. What matters is you are willing to tap the power of the eternal now and the eternal present to remake your reality. If you are looking for a way out of the estrangement struggle, frustration and anxiety follow the plan laid out by this book. You owe it to yourself.

THE END....

Or is it just the beginning???

Sheila Texeira is a retired RN, whose career was primarily in Corrections and Forensic Psych. She has been fascinated with the human mind and it's potential from the age of 10 when she watched her first stage hypnosis show.

This fascination continued well into her nursing career and into retirement when she found herself estranged from both her adult children. Wanting to turn everything into a positive, she wrote this book to help others suffering this unimaginable pain.

Sheila is married to the love of her life, Mark and owns a Boston Terrier.